The photographs of Zygmunt Bauman

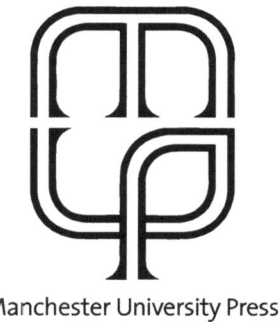

Manchester University Press

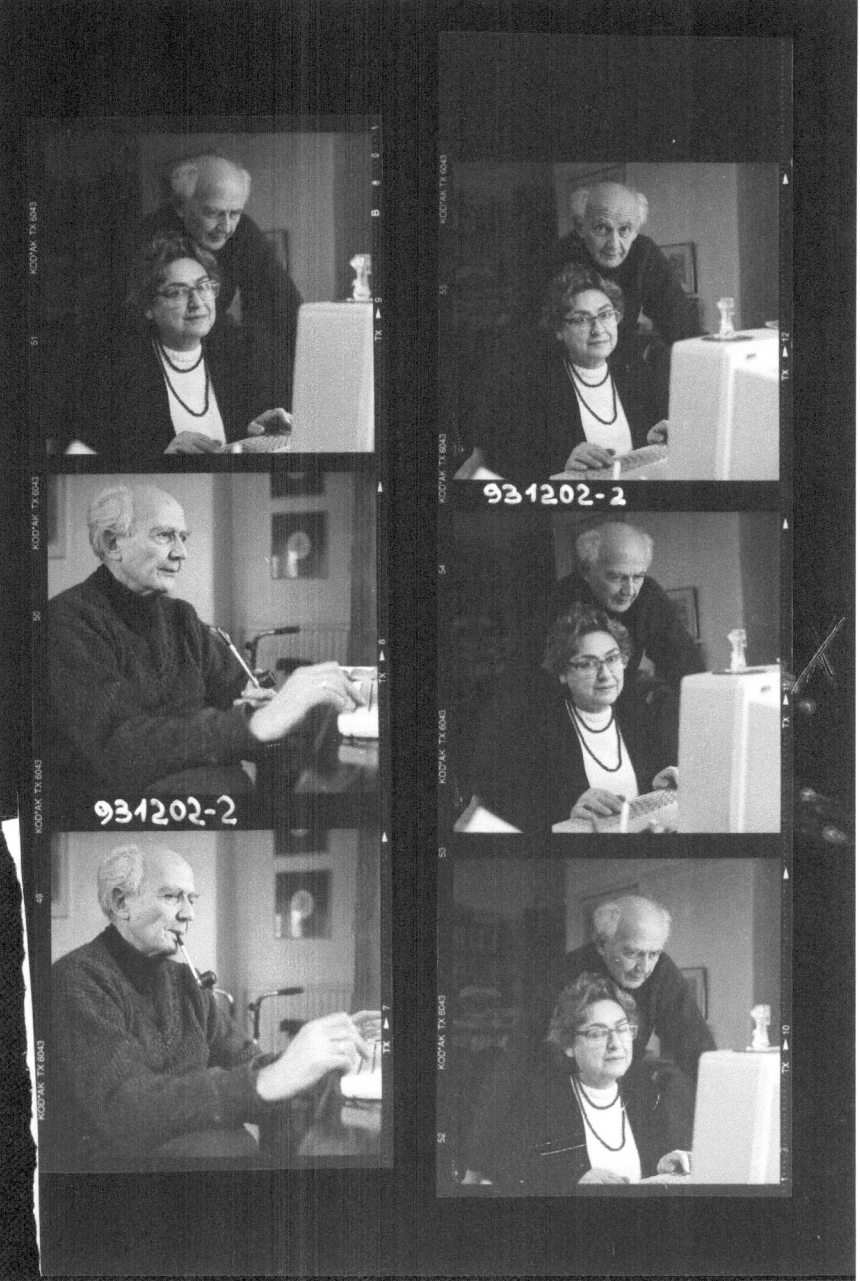

The photographs of Zygmunt Bauman

Edited by Peter Beilharz and Janet Wolff

Manchester University Press

The creation of this volume was made possible due to generous contributions from The Bauman Institute and *Thesis Eleven*

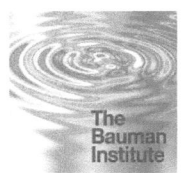 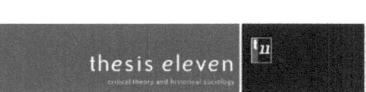

Published by Manchester University Press
Oxford Road, Manchester M13 9PL

www.manchesteruniversitypress.co.uk

British Library Cataloguing-in-Publication Data
A catalogue record for this book is available from the British Library

ISBN 978 1 5261 6842 9 paperback

First published 2023

Typeset
by Cheshire Typesetting Ltd, Cuddington, Cheshire

Contents

Introduction: the photographs of Zygmunt Bauman

Peter Beilharz and Janet Wolff

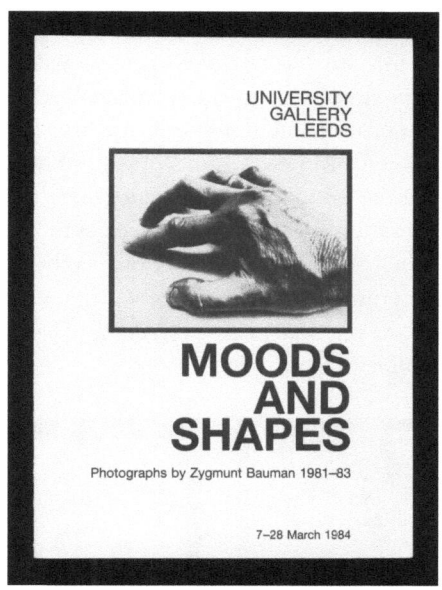

Photography is about giving shapes to moods and discovering moods in shapes. In this respect, it is not different from other visual arts or, for that matter, poetry. Like them, it positions itself between thought and feeling, things 'out there' and human experience.

Zygmunt Bauman – Foreword to an exhibition
of his photographs, February 1984

Zygmunt Bauman, internationally known and revered as the sociologist of postmodernity and of 'liquid' society, was for about a decade a serious and dedicated photographer. He explains the origin of this great enthusiasm:

I took up photography fairly recently, and virtually by accident. Travelling abroad, I used to make sketches of fine monuments of architecture that I wished to remember. But sketching took time. Worse still, looking at the products of my efforts I could not help to wonder what was so fine about my objects to inspire me in the first place. So for a trip to Germany in September 1980 I bought a compact Ricoh to do the sketching for me. Again, contemplating the bleak and dreary output of trade processing and printing, I struggled in vain to re-capture my past ecstasies. And then I saw in the window of a local photoshop a used Russian enlarger for £15. Perhaps, if I tinkered with the negatives myself, I could in the end get out from the camera exactly what went into it at the beginning.

And so, I bought the enlarger. And thus my photographic life began.[1]

He studied and learned his new craft, attending sessions at the Leeds Camera Club. He took photos of street scenes, Yorkshire views, portraits, striking juxtapositions, caught in the moment. He turned an upstairs bedroom into a studio (for portraits) and the downstairs larder into a darkroom. For about ten years, he devoted himself to this pursuit, taking his camera with him on trips (including a stay in Newfoundland) and on walks in the Yorkshire countryside. He submitted work to numerous exhibitions, and won several Certificates of Merit for his contributions (Leeds Camera Club, Yorkshire Photography Union, The Building Centre Trust, the London-based Polish Photography Society). He had solo exhibitions in different venues in Leeds as well as in Warsaw and Poznań. A letter awarding him nineteenth place in the Photography of the Year of 1986 by SLR Photography congratulates him with the words: 'You may not have quite managed to get in among the final prizewinners, but I can tell you that to finish in the top twenty is no mean feat.'

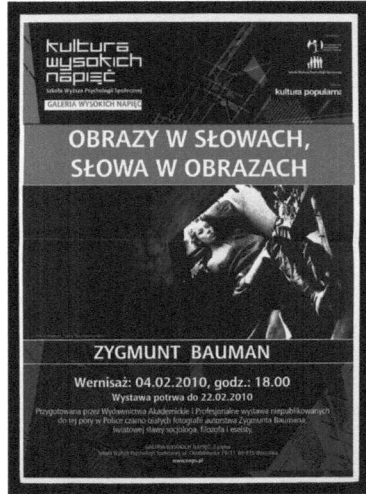 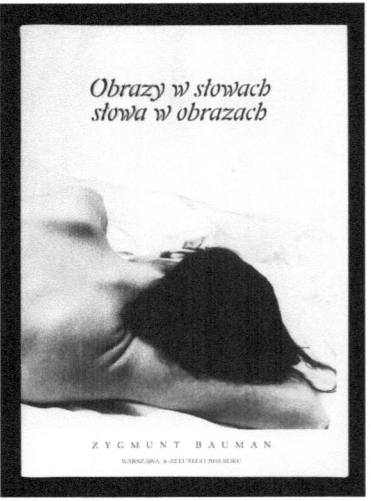

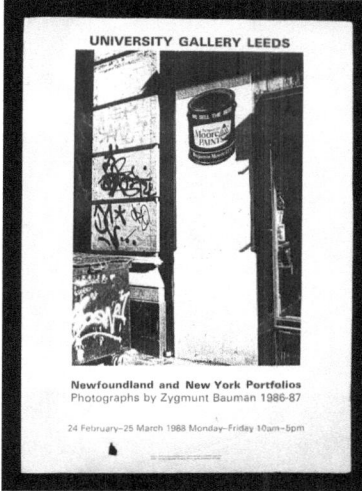

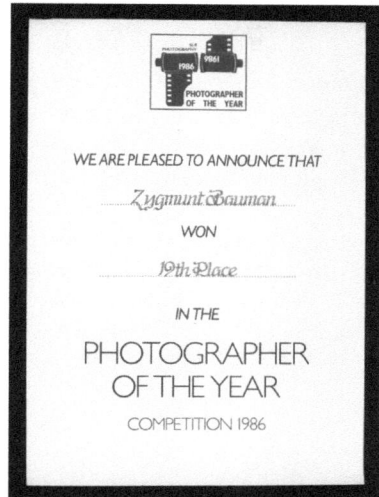

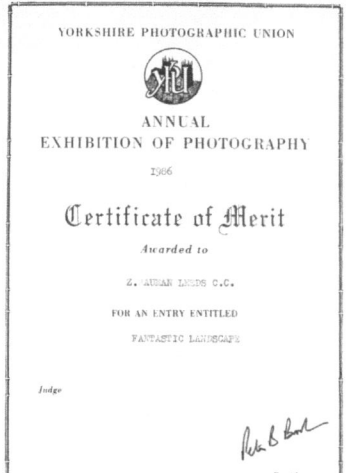

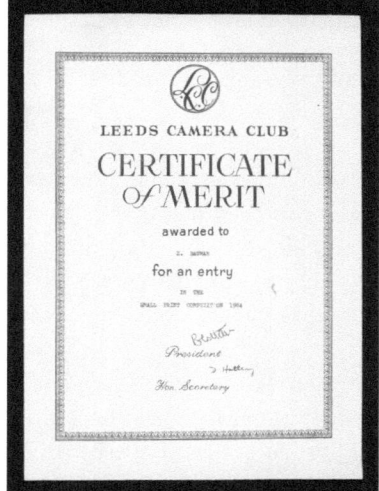

Bauman's wife Janina writes some moving words about Zygmunt's photographic practice, in her second memoir, *Dreams of Belonging* (quoted in Lydia Bauman's essay, p. 20 below):

> I watch him now, bent over his photographs, my protector, my friend, my love. His hair has turned grey, his face bears signs of a hard life, but his eyes are the same; they still burn with passion. Busy all day with his teaching, he still finds the time, strength and will to work on his new art. It came so late in his busy life, he feels he has to hurry. So, even after a tiring day, he stays up late at night to add a final touching to his unusual prints.

Although Bauman never made the case that for him photography served as a kind of sociology (though it is true that his decade of taking pictures coincided with what he thought of as his most barren period of intellectual life and production), there is no question but that his images of people – portraits or street scenes – were perceptive of character and social aspect. No great claims, but perhaps small recognitions. As he says in the same piece:

> Photography may freeze and thus make available to our reflection the apparently trivial happenings, too brief to be noticed as they occur … Once frozen into a photographic print, they stop being trivial; on the contrary; they acquire, all of a sudden, the significance of an information on the way we live; they expose the unsuspected complexity of the simplest of our relations.[2]

He wrote a good deal about the similarities between sociology and literature, often suggesting that literature may be the better observer of social life. He often gave examples of his favourite films, offering them too as brilliant perspectives on human relationships. With regard to visual art, and specifically photography, it is up to us to decide whether to read his images in such a way. (Jack Palmer, pp. 40–52 below, makes a strong and intriguing case for the complementarity of Bauman's photography and his sociological writing.)

As Bauman's biographer, Izabela Wagner, records, after about a decade he simply decided to stop. He 'explained to his family that he had reached his limits, and it interested him no more. Once he attempted to renew the activity, but the technology had advanced and Bauman was not interested in learning it.'[3] He made some late experiments with digital imagery in the early years of the new century. But his 'classic' period of photography, more or less coinciding with the 1980s, black-and-white, was over.

We began to talk about the idea of this book in September 2020. (Quite apart from anything else, it has turned out to be an excellent pandemic lockdown project for both of us.) For separate but converging reasons we were each keen to see where discussions of the photos would take us. One of us, Janet, had a long history of contact and friendship with Zygmunt and Janina Bauman. The other, Peter, had come to know the couple at a distance. Janet was an old friend, a one-time colleague and a subject of Zygmunt's photographic practice. Later, as house guest, Peter discovered the trove of photos upstairs at Lawnswood Gardens when visiting over the decades. Then there were the photos on the walls, alongside the Baumans' daughter Lydia Bauman's artwork; not much wallpaper to see, images everywhere. As it happened too, we had each recently published a memoir, moving away from academic to more personal and literary writing, and we were both enthusiastic about a new project which allowed us to engage with the aesthetic and to invite new kinds of writing.[4]

We two have in different ways long been intrigued by the image, the visual and its counterpoint to the word, that form with which intellectuals are perhaps more conventionally obsessed. Janet's work in sociology had always been in the area of the sociology of the arts. After leaving Leeds University for the USA she taught in art history (University of Rochester) and in an art school (Columbia University's School of the Arts). Peter's interest came via his engagement with the eminent Australian art historian Bernard Smith, published as *Imagining the Antipodes – Theory, Culture and the Visual in the Work of Bernard Smith* (1997), along with a longstanding interest in photography as a window onto everyday life. The relatively new fields of visual studies, visual sociology and visual anthropology were thriving, and there was a decades-long body of work in critical photography studies. The visual was, so to speak, in the air, circulating again for those of us who had an active interest in Zygmunt and Janina Bauman.

Our interest was piqued again by the first big public event sponsored by the Bauman Institute at Leeds University in 2010, and by Karl Dudman's slideshow of Zygmunt's photos for that event, which was constantly on repeat on a large screen in the main hall for those days. (Incidentally, this was the only time we two were able to meet, though the idea for this book came later.) Skype and then Zoom were well and frequently exercised in the planning and construction of this book. At about the same time, Polity Press began to publish the Bauman Institute's series of Bauman's selected writings, drawing heavily on the Bauman Archives, now held at the Brotherton Library at the University of Leeds. The first volume, on *Art and Culture*, was published in 2021 and included a portmanteau document generated by Jack Palmer out of Zygmunt's textual fragments on photography (quoted at the beginning of this introduction), as well as some reproductions of the photographs themselves.

For us, an obvious question is whether the photographs operate as a kind of sociology for Bauman, or whether we should see them as representing a complete break. We can certainly see some continuities between the images and the project of critical sociology that would later issue in the idea of liquid modernity. We can see Bauman's world, in Leeds, and elsewhere, under Thatcher in the city, and across the Yorkshire dales, as well as further afield, in Manhattan and Newfoundland. What is apparent is that Zygmunt's photographic project arrived at a moment in his professional life when for an East European exile in England sociology itself was insufficiently satisfying. His intellectual work was in some kind of hiatus. Then Janina Bauman published *Winter in the Morning*, in 1986; and Zygmunt published *Modernity and the Holocaust* in 1989. As others have pointed out, this was really a turning point for Bauman. The Holocaust opened a door to the critique of modernity, as was indicated by the first term in that book's title: *Modernity and the Holocaust*, not the other way round. It also became a moment when talk of the postmodern accelerated, and the western self-identification with the narrative of progress was again placed in serious question. The books that followed were perhaps received more as social theory or cultural studies, rather than sociology in the usual sense. There was something like a boom in social theory, and in this self-critique of modernity. This was not only instigated by the new books and their influence on other scholars, or by the seductive marketing of these by new titles by enterprising presses and fora. We ignore at our peril the question of the way in which demand also brings out supply when it comes to critical sociology. From a flatline of very little interest, Bauman became the celebrity intellectual who was expected to have views on everything, now refracted through the lens of the idea of liquid modernity. By the early 1990s, sociology had taken over again from photography in Bauman's life. (Later, around 2004, he engaged with digital photography, thanks to the gift of a digital camera from Janina.)

On his daughter Anna Sfard's suggestion we began to discuss the idea of assembling a volume featuring the photographs of Zygmunt Bauman. We were clear that the Bauman family must be involved, and quickly expanded our discussion with the three daughters to the next generation. As a result, we have contributions here from ten members of Zygmunt and Janina's family. (The grandchildren often used the Polish or Hebrew names for 'grandfather' and 'grandmother', and we have left these as written: *Dziadzia*, *Babcia*, *Saba*, *Sabta*.) A special addition here is the series of photos taken by grandson Karl Dudman in the family home (the famous 1 Lawnswood Gardens) in the week after Zygmunt's death. These are reproduced in Karl's essay, pp. 126–34 below. (A particular pleasure is to see Zygmunt's own photos reproduced in Karl's photo shots here.) We commissioned contributions from leading writers in the circle and others who knew the Baumans as family or friends.

We decided to broaden the scope of the book in two ways. The first was to include some words on Bauman's relationship to (and ideas about) film. Keith Tester, a Bauman scholar and also close friend of his, had planned, before his premature death in January 2019, a book about Bauman and film, as Peter explains in his introduction to an essay of Keith's on Bauman and Bergman, reprinted here (pp. 95–102). And, as Janina Bauman's work in postwar Poland was in the film industry, we have invited Izabela Wagner to contribute an essay on Janina and film: as Wagner has said, including in her biography of Zygmunt Bauman, it was Janina she was originally interested in, and she came to consider Zygmunt indirectly through that interest. Film was a primary interest for both of them.

The second expansion of our theme has directly to do with Janina herself. Janina and Zygmunt were married for over sixty years, from 1947 until her death in 2009. It is widely acknowledged (and explicitly stated by him) that Zygmunt's later explosion of creative intellectual work was inspired by Janina, whose memoir of her life in the Warsaw Ghetto led him in new directions, as we mention above. Therefore, as well as including material on Janina's life in film, we acknowledge two other important aspects of her life after emigration to England. First, her pottery, discussed in a short piece by her (and Zygmunt's) granddaughter, Hana Bauman-Lyons, herself an expert on studio pottery. And secondly, her research on Gypsies and Roma communities, on which she published an essay in 1998; Peter's own essay includes three of Zygmunt's photos of Gypsies. Janina's image can also be seen in three photos in the book.

In the following pages the more formal chapters and articles are interspersed with shorter untitled 'photograph essays' by family members and friends. For the latter the contributors' names appear at the end. Some of our favourite photographs were not chosen for the chapters, and we have printed these in a separate art-paper section.

Notes

1 Zygmunt Bauman, 'Thinking Photographically (1983–1985)', in Dariusz Brzeziński, Mark Davis, Jack Palmer and Tom Campbell (eds), *Zygmunt Bauman. Culture and Art. Selected Writings, Volume 1* (Cambridge: Polity Press, 2021), 103.
2 Bauman, 'Thinking Photographically', 106.
3 Izabela Wagner, *Bauman: A Biography* (Cambridge: Polity, 2020), pp. 357–8.
4 Janet Wolff, *Austerity Baby* (Manchester: Manchester University Press, 2017). Peter Beilharz, *Intimacy in Postmodern Times: A Friendship with Zygmunt Bauman* (Manchester: Manchester University Press, 2020).

Figures, images, spaces: the place of photography

Peter Beilharz

Zygmunt Bauman (1925–2017) is a household name for those who read in social theory, sociology, cultural studies. Across sixty books in English and many essays, he is widely known as the puzzler of the modern, postmodern, liquid modern and its subsets, such as liquid love. I was fortunate, together with others, to get to know him, and his wife, Janina. This necessarily meant visiting, from Australia, staying chez Bauman and entering momentarily into the everyday life cycle of Lawnswood Gardens. It meant being inserted into his household.

Bauman is not and was not widely known as a photographer. His work here is best known to his friends, as it was in a sense private, though he was sufficiently accomplished to display competitively.

What is photography? Plainly a technique, it may also be a peculiarly modern art, or even the art of modernism itself, that coming together of creativity and technology which sets it apart from other visual arts until the arrival of the installation, conceptual art and all that now fills our galleries. For Bauman, it was also a kind of home industry, or craft, and as Jack Palmer shows (pp. 40–52), may have held promise for him as an alternative to the prospect of a sociology that had, in the UK, perhaps lost its sense of adventure into the 1980s.

As Bauman's regular houseguest over many years, I had like others observed the everyday lives of the Baumans, their legendary hospitality and smoke-filled conversation, heavily heaped plates and endless snacks, talk, talk and talk. I had read their works but now also had the opportunity also to read their home, their habits and routines, observe its markers, pisa towers of books, clutters of smoking apparatus, litre bottles of duty-free, Janina's pots, cut flowers, images and artworks from the painter daughter, Lydia ... and photographs by Zygmunt Bauman. Stationed upstairs for sleep, I also had time to gaze out of the window across the playing fields, watch the traffic heading for the ring road, sleep, take in their atmosphere, read whatever manuscripts the couple would ply me with, and digest them. Lying on my back on that concave single bed, I noticed that there were piles of documents stacked loosely on top of the freestanding cupboards. The curiosity was too much. I took them down, dusty, and looked. There were hundreds of prints, of various subjects. So I asked, then, at the table, what was the story behind this trove. For I was curious, of course, but also immediately suspicious that these would matter, that they would offer some other window to knowing Zygmunt Bauman. He was dismissive of his work in photography, past tense; but then he did not like to talk about his writing, either, only the ideas that animated us together.

Around the same time, I began regularly to visit my relatives near Stuttgart. It was another journey of discovery. Hitherto I had pushed Germany away, unable to look the burden of Nazism in the face. They shared their hospitality with me, showed me family solidarity and kindness, but also of their wisdom, and wit when they said to me they had worked out what I was up to. I had no idea what they were talking about; *keine Ahnung*. They laughed. The joke was on me. They had worked out that I visited to take notes: surely I was writing a book about them, after all I was a sociologist. Intuitively they had understood the idea of longitudinal research. But no; I observed, as I was keen to know what I could of their way of life, but did not look to make of them a case study.

Nor the Baumans; but when Zygmunt died and my grief was protracted, I began to write it out. I wrote a memoir, later to be published as *Intimacy in Postmodern Times* (2020).[1] I shared the manuscript with the family, as a matter of courtesy, but also looking to prevent howlers. This was a new departure for me as a writer, involving among other things something that felt like disclosure. Anna Sfard responded rather that I seemed to know the couple very well. This came as a relief. But then, what about those photos, which I had mentioned in my book, and indeed included some that Bauman took of me and my son in a later, digital moment around 2004?

Zygmunt had chastised me on the one previous occasion after 2007 when I had written, or rather published, about life at Lawnswood Gardens.[2] It was as though I had breached his privacy. I had wanted to share the image of his own intense humanity. Relieved of the presence of his scrutiny after his death in 2017, I now took a moment to write about his photographs. But Anna was sug-gesting more, that I should consider turning to the Bauman Institute Archive as a source to write further. I took the liberty of writing to Janet Wolff, whose work I had always admired, as well as her expertise in the visual, so much more than my own. She had just published her *Austerity Baby* project, a wonderful crossover of the visual and the social.[3] We were heading perhaps in a similar direction, where personal was historical and social if less directly political in the sense championed on the left since the 1960s. More, she had known Zygmunt and Janina in the period of his most earnest photographic activity, around 1980–88, and had indeed been his subject for several portraits.

Perhaps we might contemplate the idea of sharing such a project? (Here, in any case, are the results!)

There were other prompts. Earlier I had discussed Bauman's photos with Chris Rojek, who had used an image by Zygmunt of Manhattan street life for the cover of one book he published by Bauman, *Intimations of Postmodernity*.[4] I had heard other stories, about the Baumans travelling afar in Newfoundland for example, and even as far away as Australia. In the meantime, I became familiar with the photos of J.M. Coetzee, and Pierre Bourdieu; and I had written together with Sian Supski about the work of the Australian photographer Carol Jerrems.[5] The history of photography and everyday life, cities and rock-music photos intrigued me. I touched passingly on this iceberg topic in my memoir, including photos Bauman took of me and my son, Nikolai. Bauman had been gifted a digital device by Janina, after a long time away from the camera. He was sceptical of useless progress, but was also interested in gadgets, giving me a micro-recorder as a gift. 'Do you like gadgets?' He was fascinated by the tricks you could now perform with digital photography, like Paintbox, which he used on a number of images of us, as shown here:

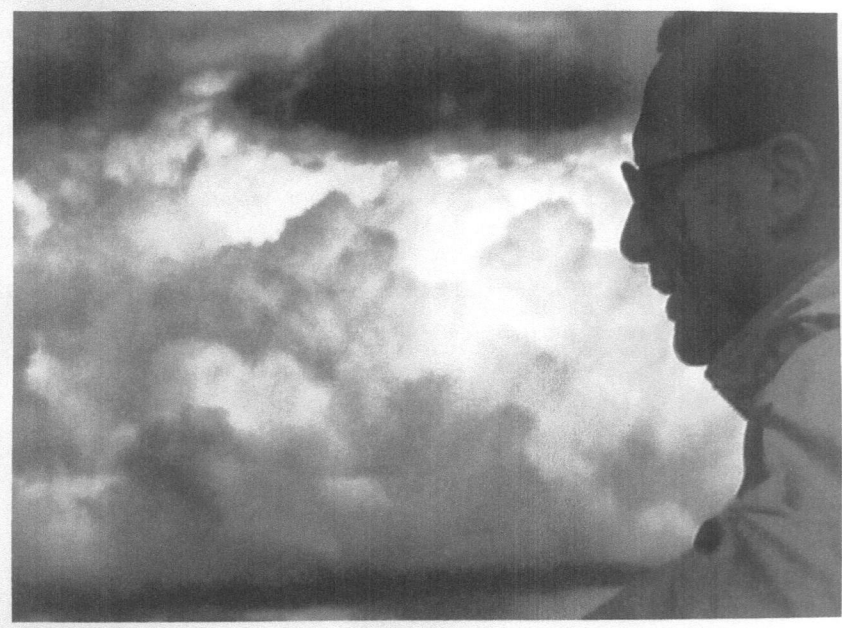

Bauman had other distractions. In this period, 1985–2008, for example, he wrote copious book reviews. Here is a research project for another day, or hand: Bauman as reviewer. This is uncommon; as intellectuals become stellar they usually expect to be reviewed, but not to write reviews themselves. He was always a ravenous reader and consumer of news and images alike.

Into this period the Bauman Institute team began to develop their project for a three-volume series of Bauman's selected writings, Mark Davis then as director and Jack Palmer as archival driver. Jack assembled the available fragments of text on photography into a single piece, editorially entitled 'Thinking Photographically (1983–1985)' and reproducing several images.[6] There Bauman refers to three masters, Cartier-Bresson, Kertesz and Brandt. The horizons of his interests were both slow/aesthetic, and quick/streetwise. Bauman was to exhibit competitively in the UK and in Europe. Recent enthusiasts for his work got a glimpse of his portfolio in a flipshow organised by Karl Dudman for the Bauman Institute launch event in 2010, these images shown together with a catalogue, *Pictures in Words, Words in Pictures*.

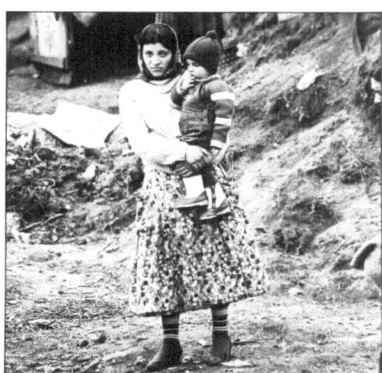 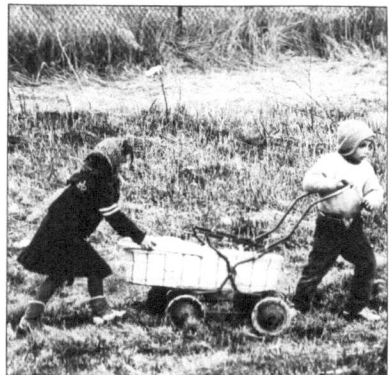

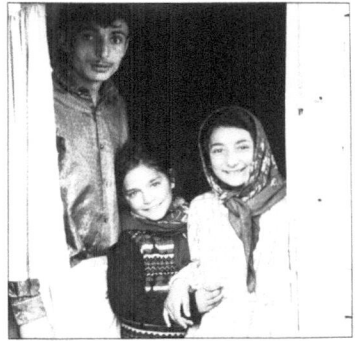

What then were Bauman's frames, or ways of seeing or viewing? There were the portraits, both posed – singular and in couples – and snapped on the street or in the park. There were the studies of other people's lives, the Romany, and the inhabitants of Manhattan. Janina had written about the Gypsies or Romany as 'Demons of Other People's Fears' in a piece we published in *Thesis Eleven*.[7] Zygmunt's interest seems to be in the everyday life setting of his subjects, but also in their faces. They appear as actors, rather than as victims. Sometimes they smile. Bauman seems often given, or at least responsive, to other forms of coupling, as in the photos of the local churchyard or Skidoo included in this book, where two figures are captured as they collide or enter each other's orbits, or else just pass each other by. Much of this work could be called dirty realism. Its motifs are early Thatcher, sleeping rough, doing it tough, empty promises of consumer dreams read against their daily reality; these souls are among the collateral damage of postmodern times. This new world that is also an old world, for the down and out. Indeed, they read like a visual critique of Thatcherism and its effects, in terms of what Tom Hazeldine more recently in echo of Gramsci has called *The Northern Question*.[8] The landscapes also vary. Yorkshire, frequently, wild and still, sometimes built, sometimes in ruins; fences, boundaries, seating, children; sandalled stockinged feet and small dogs, but also the sublime in Newfoundland, the latter slow, and striking, as Palmer observes. My friend the Australian photographer Ian North said of these Newfoundland images that they would each have taken a day, all day, waiting for the proverbial light. Ian also drew our attention to the period use of irony, or juxtaposition, as in the prosperity and poverty thrown together in those Thatcherist works. Not just street messages, these are also mixed messages, and messages about the mixed modernities of tourists and vagabonds, parvenus and pariahs. There were the nudes, part of the period male portfolio, varying from some closer to his enthusiasm for Bill Brandt, a suggestive parallel also with a shared Yorkshire moment, to others like the solarisation effect of Man Ray rather earlier in the twentieth century. The echoes of Brandt in particular in Bauman's work are telling, and are also suggestive for further prospective research and examination. You could easily take one for the other, even if Brandt has the edge.

Then there are figures of modernity, those out of place or displaced. Not without its classical resonances in landscapes, Bauman's work is also given to the pedestrian. The sociology of everyday life takes its co-ordinates into photography of everyday life. Finally, there is what we might call documentary realism. These images are not included here, as they are illustrative, and poorly reproduced, but they remain suggestive of Bauman's interests and motivations. They are to be found, for example in the now obscure small book published in 1984 as a Barnardo Practice Work Paper as *Osmondthorpe – The Area that Time Forgot*.[9]

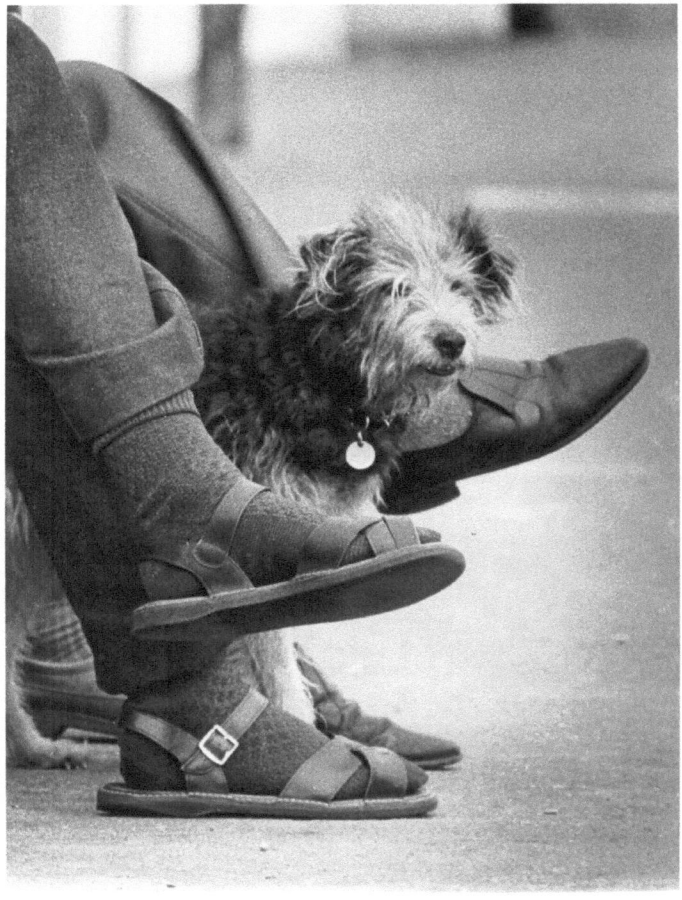

This is a study of an interwar council estate east of central Leeds by Alan Wolinski. Wolinski thanks Ziggy Bauman for the photos. It is a fascinating book, a critique of the kind of planning that left people and community ties and places out of consideration. Lacking any centre, the town is dormitory but at the same time a welfare town. There is no community space, and no community. There is serious poverty and serious waste of human lives. Empty spaces, and young people with spirit smiling straight at the camera and the balding Pole behind it. These may not be the most interesting of his photos, and they are poorly rendered in book form, but they are nevertheless suggestive of his willingness to document, to give witness with a camera. His subjects, like the Romany or the Leeds boys on bikes, offer signs of life.

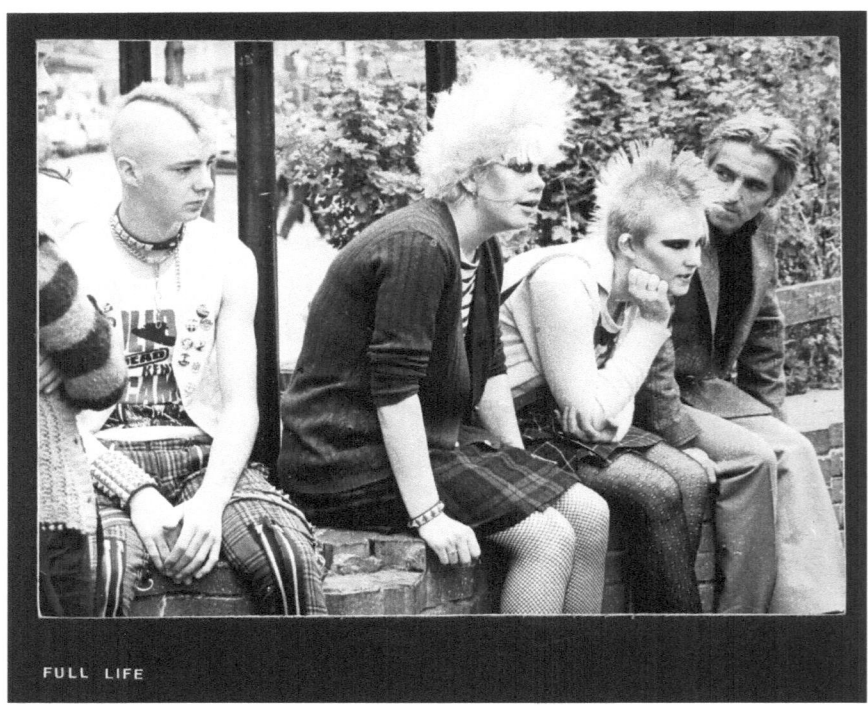

FULL LIFE

How are we to begin to make sense of all this? Were sociology and photography alternatives in Bauman's life, or corresponding streams? This period
into the 1980s represents a fascinating moment in Bauman's intellectual career,
in the life of his mind. The peculiar profile of the émigré, the exile, was often
taken in the time of the Cold War to be by definition anti-communist. What
were his wares, when Bauman left Poland? And what was the sociological
world he entered? He had been trained, in his second life as an academi-
cian, in Continental philosophy and sociology. His mentors, scholars such as
Hochfeld, Schaff and Ossowski, were of some influence in Europe but were
little known in the USA, which dominated the world scene in terms of size, critical mass and resources. Bauman came to Leeds armed with phenomenology,
Schutz, Simmel's stranger, and a wad of reading in American sociology and
anthropology. He had some friends and colleagues, other refugees like Elias,
Kołakowski, and Hirszowitz, and was finding enthusiasm from the younger
generation around him in Leeds. Bauman was a well-known enthusiast for hermeneutics, which was effectively eclipsed by structuralism and French theory.
He was an ambivalent fellow traveller of the Frankfurt School, but his was an
East European Marxism, even as it crossed paths with the Weberian strain of
the Budapest School.[10]

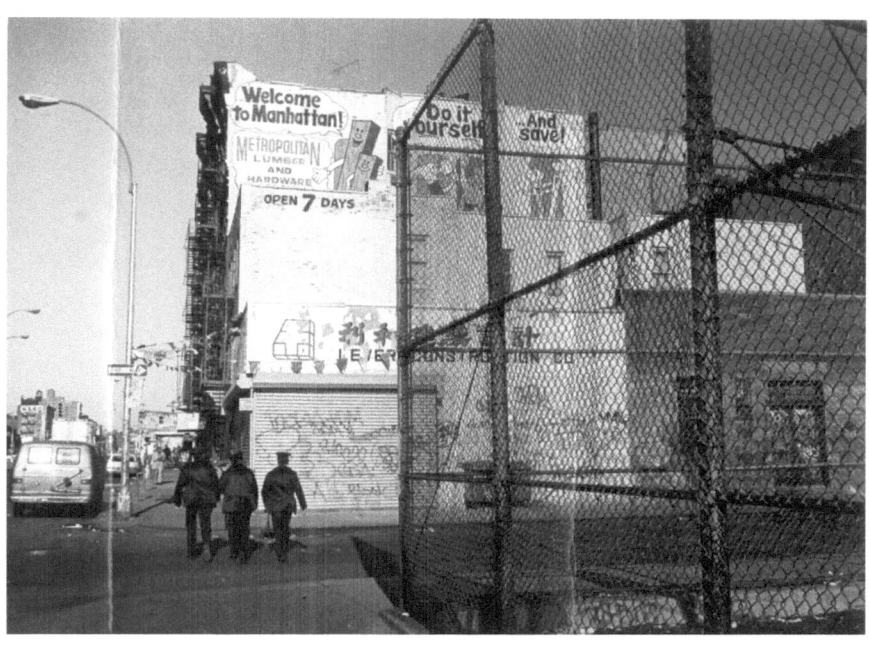

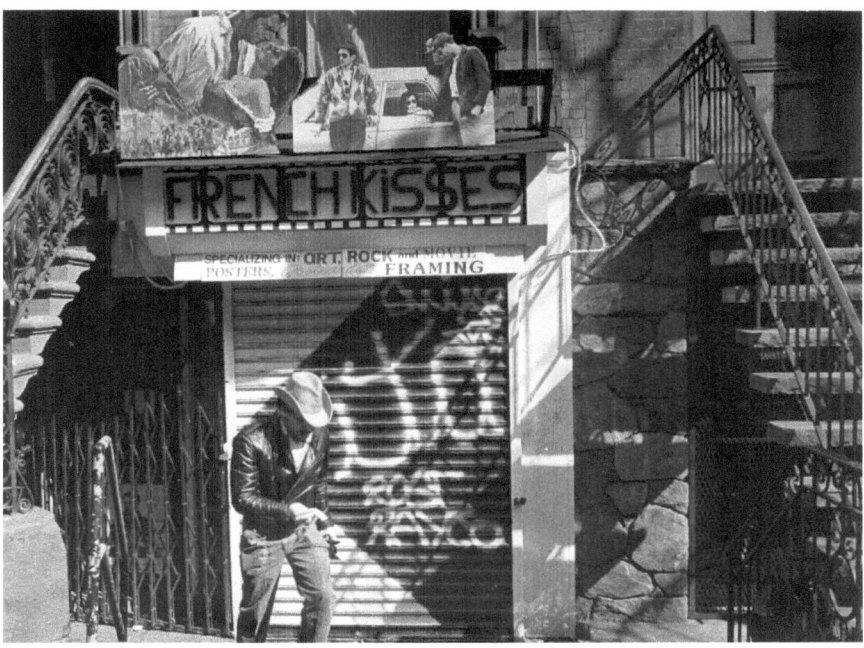

Bauman used to rag me for attending big events like the annual Proceedings of the American Sociological Association. Six thousand sociologists in one place was his image of hell. As he would opine, perhaps echoing his father, 'I have nothing to sell, nor am I looking to buy'. He was not a careerist, but he did need to make a living in a new land, and to follow his intellectual heart. It seems likely that photography emerged in the 1980s as a kind of intellectual and personal lifeline in this situation, where he was placed yet simultaneously displaced. Whatever the case, this was Bauman before Bauman. Nobody knew at this point, in the 1980s, that his would become that household name. There he was, with Janina and his family in Leeds, doing sociology by day and photography by night, making a living, and still hoping that it might be possible to change the world, even perhaps in the age of Thatcher. Or maybe not. The space of politics was also shrinking.

My sense is that the project of photography arrived in this hiatus, where his Polish or East European intellectual identity as a new critical theorist had been put on hold, as he failed easily to find an independent place in the English scene. He was a professor, with high status, but maybe the wrong kind of professor; and he wished to profess, but he was also kind of invisible. This must be one of the hardest costs to pay for exile, especially exile on a one-way exit visa. Go! he had been told by the Polish state, which he had also helped to establish in the model of socialist Poland, as soldier, citizen and social scientist. Never return! he was told. He had been stripped of his professional identity, as well as his citizenship; and, as it has been observed, he would never have been a Polish sociologist in Poland anyway; there, he was a Jewish sociologist, depending on which way the wind might blow. It is apparent that he was disillusioned and disappointed with what passed for English sociology, a discipline with which he was also pistol-whipped by E.P. Thompson.[11] The apparent alternative, *New Left Review*, had no place for or interest in Bauman. The English left had difficulties placing these exiles, committed as the locals often still were to some kind of residual defence of the legacy of Soviet-type societies. But in the 1980s new intellectual doors were hewn out, or opened up. There was revival of past precedents of radical thinking, and space for non-Soviet enthusiasms for socialism.

Zygmunt Bauman did not want to be a Sovietologist; he remained a socialist. And this is one reason among others that he found the idea of working in the United States unattractive; there, this would be a straitjacket he would be unable to escape. He did write once for *Problems of Communism*; but only once, in 1971. This was to remain a path not taken.

What were these new doors? There are some several, and they seem somehow to coalesce. There were new networks of friends in radical journals; and there was his new emerging book platform, a place from which to speak, with the Polity Press.

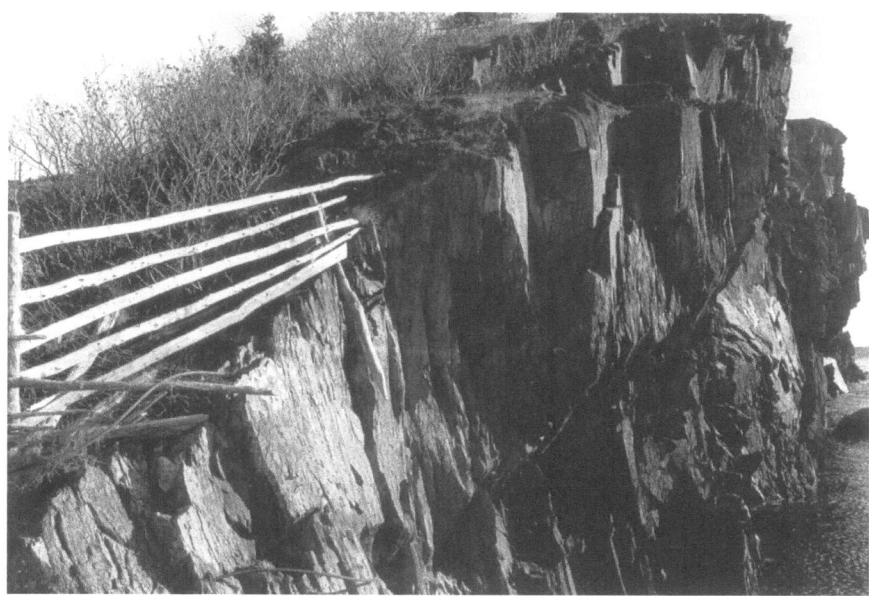

Telos was born in 1968 as an American new left journal of phenomenological and Hegelian Marxism. It became a first port of call for readers interested in critical theory, western Marxism, and the alternative views of Castoriadis and Lefort, the Budapest School, and thinkers like Zygmunt Bauman, as well as other émigrés like Zaslavsky. Bauman published in *Telos* in 1981, 1986, 1988 and 1989. Especially significant was the brilliant interview with Bauman published in *Telos* in 1992, which did much to profile the breadth and extent of his work for English speakers. Whatever support and succour Bauman received in Leeds, this was a network full of promise for him. Led by Paul Piccone, an explosive editor and shaker sometimes referred to as its own red dictator, *Telos* was also a small social movement of sorts, sustained by a network of *Telos* groups such as those in Buffalo, St Louis, Kansas, Toronto, etc.

There was, incidentally, a *Telos* group in Newfoundland, where the Baumans stayed on sabbatical in 1986. Piccone had worked there earlier, as Alan Sica reminds us, around 1981.[12] There was some significant influence here. Bauman thanks Zaslavsky, Piccone and a number of the *Telos* crew in *Legislators and Interpreters* (1987) as well as Tony Giddens. It was his debut with the emergent Polity Press. He signs off 'Leeds – St Johns [*sic*]'. As Jack Palmer suggests (pp. 43–7 below), Bauman seems to have found intellectual lift in both the place and the people there. It was a cusp, but its further meaning remained as yet unclear.

Thesis Eleven is another story, which overlaps with his relationship with me as its founding editor. *Thesis Eleven* was born in 1980 in Melbourne. Feher and

Heller, Davidson and others were key formative influences. Gramsci and Lukács were our early lodestars; historical sociology and critical theory our destinations. David Roberts first commissioned Bauman to write for *Thesis Eleven* in 1989, after I had invited him to join the editorial advisory board in 1988. The trigger here, again, was Bauman's adventure into the postmodern, *Legislators and Interpreters*. Zygmunt published in *Thesis Eleven* in 1989, 1991, 1992, 1995, 2002, 2010, 2013, Janina in 1998 and 2001. This was another home.

Theory, Culture and Society was established in 1982 and has become a standard reference for social and cultural theory. Originally under the auspices of Mike Featherstone, but working with a cast of thousands, it brought together all manner of British and European thinkers and writers in social theory and cultural studies. It opened out on to different worlds. Bauman published in the journal in 1983, 1985, 1988, 1990, 1992, 2000, 2002, 2004.

Polity Press was established at Oxford by Tony Giddens and David Held in 1984. It was then and is now an incredible project of translation, commissioning and publicity for European social theory, and including Giddens at the height of his powers, as in *The Constitution of Society* (1984).[13] This was to become a welcome home for Bauman, who with John Thompson as chief editor became a regular Polity person. Obviously all these avenues involved affirmation, as Bauman himself became globalised.

My point is simple: Bauman's life was also a part of the process he analysed, the path we came to call globalisation. Suddenly, if yet slowly, his audience and his interlocutors expanded dramatically, and his message no longer fell out of the reception process. Into the 1980s Bauman shifted from the Polish/Anglo social-sciences community into the emerging global social-theory community. Thus Bauman became European, as well as East European and an exile, and more, his influence spread globally. Bauman was part himself of the globalisation process that he was also trying to make sense of. Photography, which he said he initially gave up because of the cost of developing, gave way to the growing frenzy of writing and speaking around his part of the globe, with time in Lawnswood Gardens as respite. The photographs featured across the pages of this book rest within the period of apparent disillusion with the practice of mainstream sociology which then gave way to the accelerations of the globalisation process and the postmodern, then liquid modern turn.

This was a world continuous with, and yet miles away from, his everyday life of the 1980s. By now he was no longer the snapper. What you may find in these pages tells of other worlds and optics. In Leeds he had opened the aperture. Now he was beckoned, again, by the power of the word. His days with the camera remain intriguing, as this volume shows. The images remain.

Notes

1 Peter Beilharz, *Intimacy in Postmodern Times: A Friendship with Zygmunt Bauman* (Manchester: Manchester University Press, 2020).

2 Beilharz, *Intimacy*, 54–8.

3 Janet Wolff, *Austerity Baby* (Manchester: Manchester University Press, 2017).

4 Zygmunt Bauman, *Intimations of Postmodernity* (London: Routledge, 1991).

5 Beilharz and Sian Supski, 'Tricks with Mirrors – Sharpies and Their Representations', in S. Baker, B. Robards and B. Buttigieg (eds), *Youth Cultures and Subcultures* (London: Routledge, 2015); Beilharz and Supski, 'So Sharp You Could Bleed – Sharpies and Their Representations', in A. Michelsen and F. Tygstrup (eds), *Socioaesthetics* (Leiden: Brill, 2015).

6 Zygmunt Bauman, *Culture and Art* (Oxford: Polity, 2021), 103–11. And see generally Jack Palmer, *Zygmunt Bauman and the West* (Montreal: McGill-Queen's University Press, 2023).

7 Janina Bauman, 'Demons of Other People's Fears', *Thesis Eleven*, 54 (1998).

8 Tom Hazeldine, *The Northern Question* (London: Verso, 2020).

9 Alan Wolinski, *Osmondthorpe – The Area that Time Forgot. A Study of Community Work on an Inter-war Council Estate* (Hertford: Dr Barnardo's, 1984).

10 Beilharz, *Intimacy*, 126–9.

11 Beilharz, 'Zygmunt Bauman – Weberian Marxist', in M.H. Jacobsen (ed.), *Anthem Companion to Zygmunt Bauman* (London: Anthem, 2023).

12 Alan Sica, 'Knowing the Unknowable Paul Piccone', *Fast Capitalism*, 5.1 (2009), MAVS Open Press.

13 Anthony Giddens, *The Constitution of Society* (Oxford: Polity, 1984).

Pictures in words, words in pictures (2010)

Lydia Bauman

I watch him now, bent over his photographs, my protector, my friend, my love. His hair has turned grey, his face bears signs of a hard life, but his eyes are the same: they still burn with passion. Busy all day with his teaching, he still finds the time, strength and will to work on his new art. It came so late in his busy life, he feels he has to hurry. So, even after a tiring day, he stays up late at night to add a final touching to his unusual prints.

Dripping wet from wash, the photographs show the austere beauty of the Yorkshire landscape, a beauty of stillness and solitude. How does he see such sadness among those green valley and hills? and why does he search for it?

Janina Bauman, *A Dream of Belonging* (London: Virago, 1988)

By the time my mother wrote these words, I was no longer living at home, but I do remember the beginnings of my father's passion for photography. I remember him darting between the fizzing vats of home-made wine ranged along the radiator of the breakfast room, and the pantry, where in the company of sticky jam jars and breakfast cereals, he performed his alchemies in the dark.

This utter lack of pretentiousness in the act of creating was entirely in keeping with a man who shaped his staggering intellectual output in a broom-cupboard of a room, perched on a hard chair and hunched over a modest typewriter littered with pipe tobacco.

I remember the sense of surprise when, on visiting my parents in years that followed, I would encounter the results of these early experiments, framed up and hung along the length of the staircase leading from the hall to the upper floor. I was startled by their 'out of nowhere' maturity, their very idiosyncratic mood and the sheer aesthetic pleasure they gave. That my father had an artistic bent, I had no doubt. I had seen his drawings in charcoal, which he made over a short period in the 1970s, inspired by one old master or another. I know how profoundly art, be it painting or music or literature, affects him. And I know the depth of his conviction when he first encouraged and then supported my own lifelong engagement with painting.

But photography, pile upon tangible pile and sustained hours of it, came as a surprise.

It seemed to be born fully formed, of some immaculate conception, as perhaps one would expect from a man of my father's fierce independence. Looking at them through the eyes of an art historian, accustomed to searching for trends, links, influences, I can only see him.

I am struck by a sense of his presence in those, often desolate, scenes. I can get a measure both of his own separateness and of his eye trained upon his subject, his mind working. These images speak with his voice. It is an eloquent voice which is clear, but whose message is multi-layered, subtle, ironic, witty.

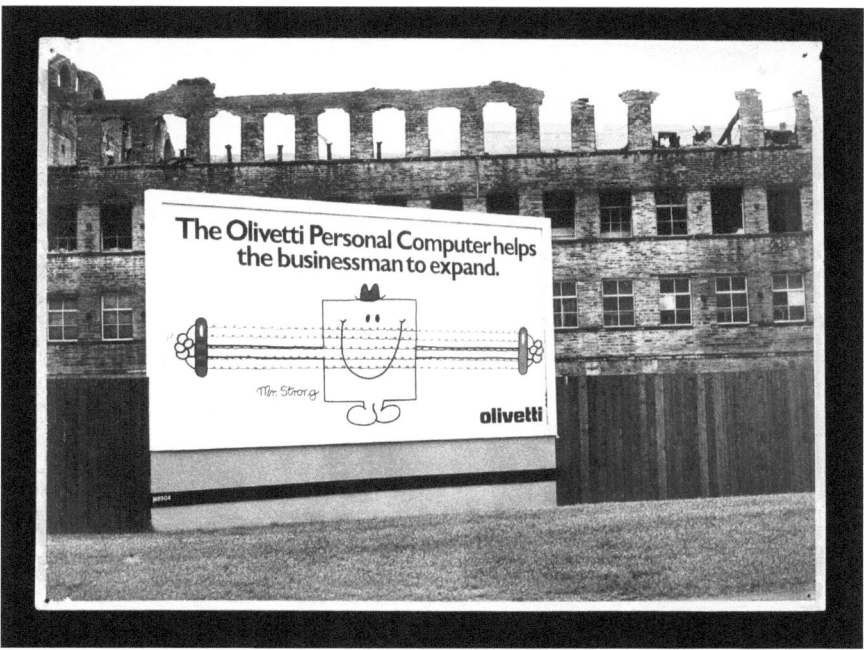

Take 'The Olivetti Personal Computer Helps the Businessman to Expand'. Not only is there an obvious irony in the juxtaposition of a billboard advertising some cutting-edge gadget with the derelict scene, but the jolly Mr Strong figure flexing his cartoon muscles chimes in with the vision of gladiatorial exploits evoked by the faintly Colosseum-like structure of the building behind. On a visual level, the arm exerciser, which he stretches impossibly wide, picks up on the endless progression of brooding, broken windows. A comment perhaps, on the futility of human endeavour.

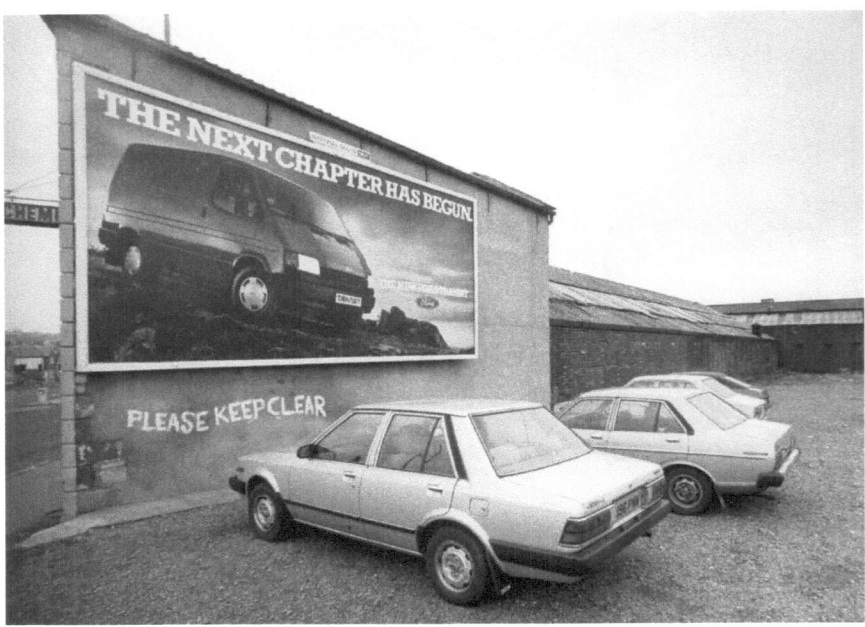

Or consider 'The Next Chapter Has Begun' and the senseless insubordination of a row of beat-up cars under a bleak and uneventful sky, pressing against a blind wall bearing a scrawled sign 'Please Keep Clear'. Nose to nose with a powerful new model which looks down on them from a billboard, gleaming under the animated sky and corporate logo and clearly going places across a challenging and adventurous terrain, these cars are going nowhere. No such Next Chapter will begin for them any time soon. They make us think of the ultimate pointlessness of rebellion against authority, of social inequality, of the haves and have-nots both in material terms and in terms of the prospects afforded by life.

And then again the scene of three groups of people so locked in their own worlds that they seem unaware of the others, a common enough phenomenon, but captured here by the metaphor of turned backs, repetition of faceless figures, entangled bodies. As the trio of teenagers facing an impenetrable thicket of vegetation gives way to lovers in the foreground and a mature couple strolling engrossed out of the picture, we are made to think of the stages of life, spent together but apart.

Pessimism and melancholy underlying these visions will be familiar to all Bauman readers.

But here they are tempered by a formal beauty, common to his city, land and bodyscapes, a beauty residing in the old pictorial tradition of balanced

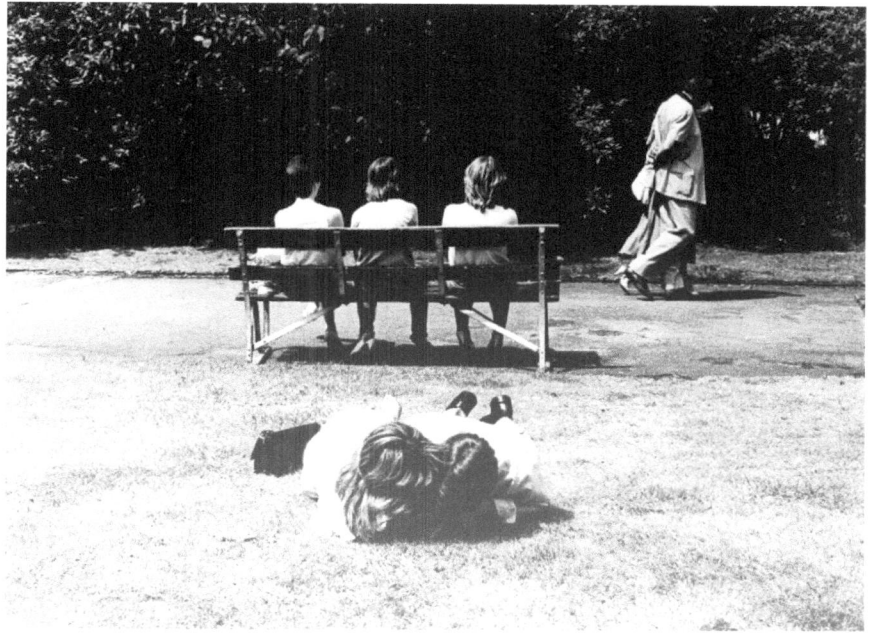

compositions, dramatic *chiaroscuro*, repetition of patterns, the interplay of lush velvety blacks with luminous whites unique to photography. It is this formal beauty which ultimately divests these pessimistic messages of their didactic or judgmental intent. They become musings, timeless meditations on the way things are, with no design other than to capture chance encounters mid-flight as they occur and to do so with an eye for aesthetic integrity. In that sense they mirror their creator's mind – constantly thoughtful but always receptive and quick to capture what is all around us and transform it into something startling, eloquent and brilliant.

My father's photographs still hang the length of the wall above the stairs. They were always intended to remain private. They were the last images that my mother could still enjoy close up on her slow, majestic ascent up the stair lift in the last months of her life.

Brought out in public view, they will reveal that for Zygmunt Bauman photography is as potent a medium as the written word. It is indeed a case of 'pictures in words and words in pictures'.

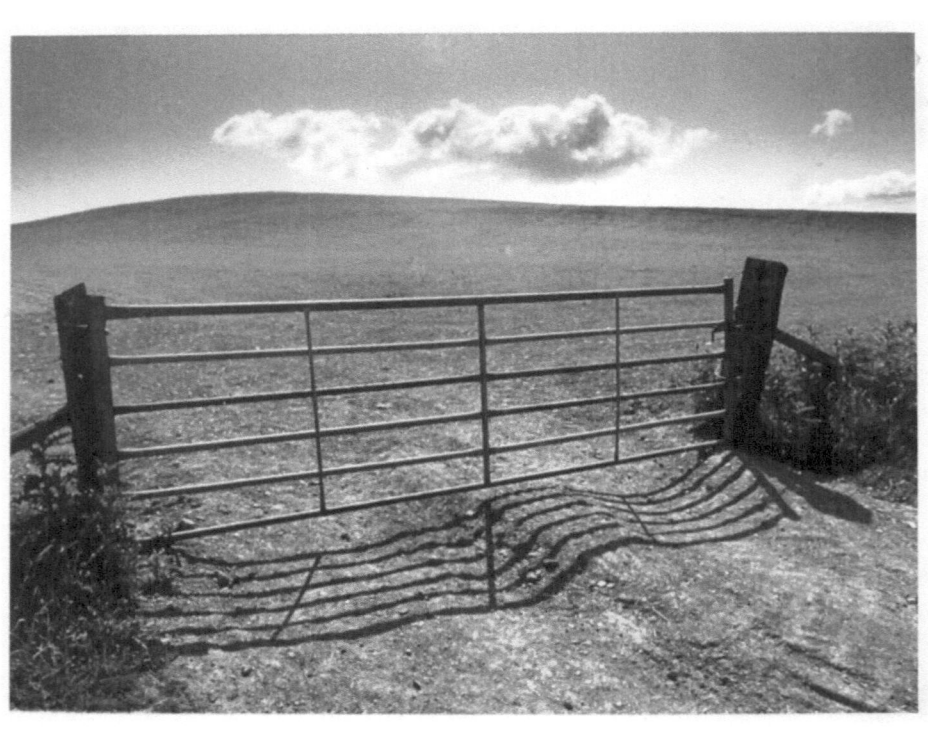

I was ten years old or so when I first saw this photograph. I remember *Dziadzia* discussing it with someone, probably with one of my parents. He quoted words of an acquaintance whose connoisseur opinion he evidently held in high respect. According to that person, the image would have been better if it showed the gate ajar rather than completely shut. As much as *Dziadzia* valued the expert's criticism, he would not yield. He was happy with the picture as it was. He passionately argued in its defence, repeating what the critic said only to dismiss it forcefully with well substantiated claims.

Forty years later, I examine the photograph with different eyes. It was taken by a person who experienced two authoritarian regimes and a world war, who fought fascism and nationalism and who, together with his family, became a stateless refugee, and not just once, but twice. The image was created by the man who, observing the future of humankind in an interview, said he was a pessimist for the short term and an optimist for the long term. As I am re-inspecting the picture these days, the roads of Europe are once again flooded with hundreds of thousands of refugees, and I ask myself, what does the closed gate mean? It is suddenly not clear to me whose gaze is depicted in the picture – that of a person who yearns to cross the gate towards a greener future *outside*, or that of a guard, protecting the *inside* from an alien invasion? And is the field on the *other* side really so much greener? After all, the picture is in black-and-white and the beds of green grass I see on the other side may be saying more about me than about the reality beyond the gate. On second thoughts, even the white cloud may not be as harmless as it initially seemed to me. In fact, it may herald a storm. Indeed, now I notice that its right part is ominously dark.

Why did *Dziadzia* leave the gate closed?

A closed gate signals an act of separation. The photographer is by no means an external observer – he is there, standing on the road in front of the gate, his gaze turned towards the other side. You cannot tell whether the photographer is 'in' or 'out'. Actually, composition alone cannot by itself render such categorisations because they demand political judgement that is external to the documented objects. Designating a zone as *in* or *out* depends on where one wants to go and who is denied the right to do so. Does a photograph with a closed gate at its centre indeed invoke such denial and separation?

Unlike a wall or a fence, a gate – by its very nature – can be opened. This, I think, is the reason why *Dziadzia* chose to leave it closed. Opening the gate is possible, maybe even easy, but doing this requires a political and moral act. It demands a human act.

Michael Sfard

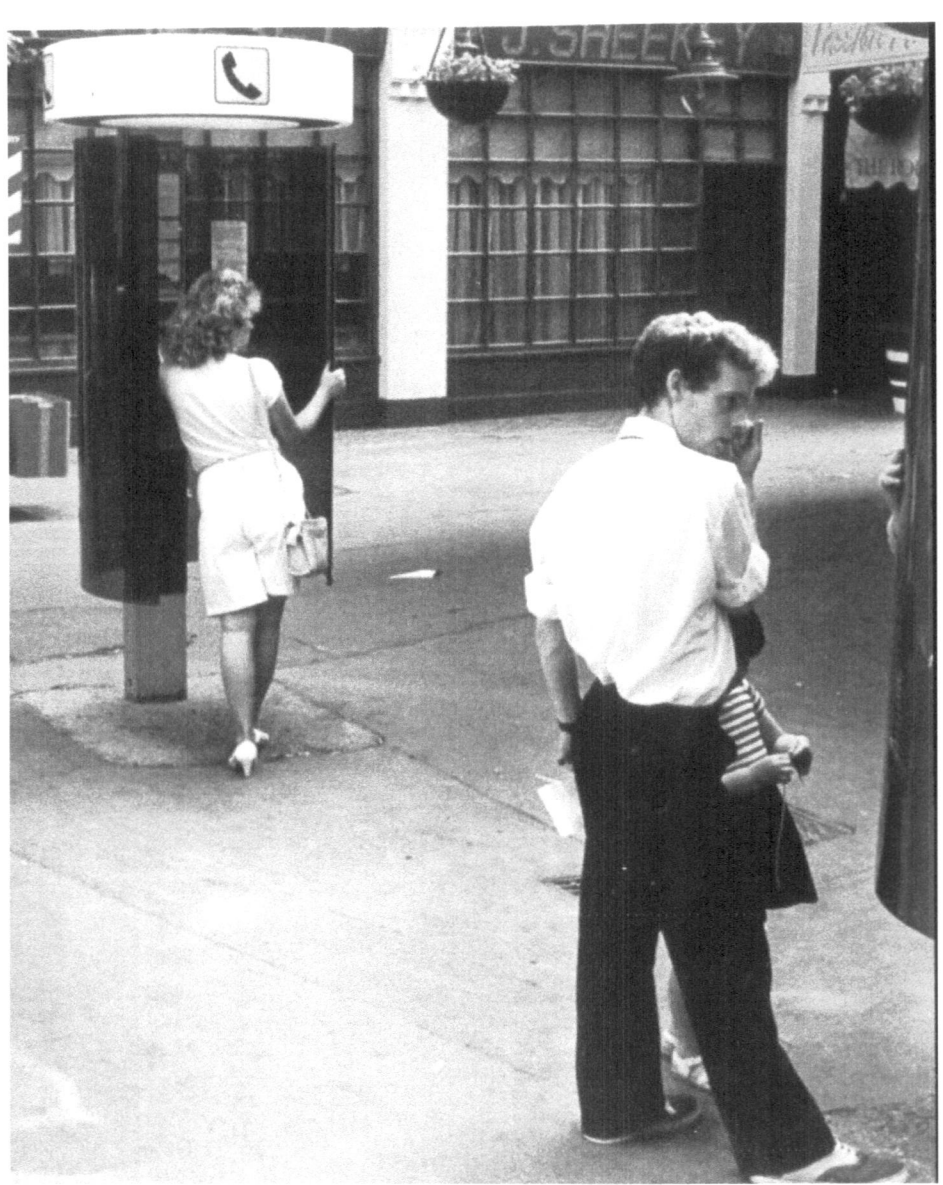

It is a street scene. The light clothes of the people in the photograph suggest it is summer. The observed are unaware of being photographed. They are going about their business—making phone calls before mobile phones, not in an iconic GPO red callbox, but a European-type rotunda of open booths, post-privatisation (1981). We can identify the location of this photograph from the banner, J. Sheekey, a famous fish and seafood restaurant founded in 1895 in the theatre district of London, off St Martin's Lane. Was the occasion for the photograph a trip to London to go to the theatre? What drew the photographer's attention to this scene? Was it the rear view of the woman with curly hair all dressed in white, culottes with high heels, one hand resting on the structure, her body slightly twisting, looking away as she talked? What of the off-centre pair lower right? We notice a young white man, curly hair, white shirt, sleeves rolled up, dark trousers and two-tone shoes. Through his legs we glimpse the white-sandalled feet of a girl-child standing beside him in striped T-shirt and skirt, fiddling with a piece of string – bored, waiting, like him. The metal edge of another phone station with disembodied fingers clasping its metal sides explains. Two random people on the phone, one invisible with her family, another woman all dressed up, alone. Who are they phoning?

The clothes also suggest the early 1980s – no trainers and the man has hair unstyled. The image belongs to the long-established genre of street photography. It registers also as masculine *flânerie*, 'botanising on the asphalt' as Baudelaire put it. The *flâneur's* masculine gaze was/is, however, always erotic, as here. Or is it dispassionate social investigation of street folk and city life? Both. We name it an instance of *the sociological gaze*.

How did Zygmunt Bauman come to be taking photographs of random people he encountered on the street? Here is a clue. In 1978, Tony Bryant arrived in Leeds, appointed to a one-year Lectureship in Sociology. The University instituted its very first Open Day in 1979, inviting the local population to find out what each department did. Aidan Foster-Carter and Bob Towler were in charge of the Sociology department's display. How could you *show* Sociology to visitors? It was decided that photographs of different types of houses and religious buildings might do the job. Bryant, a keen photographer, set off with Towler to capture the social face of Leeds. The visitors thronged to Sociology's captivating display. Did this event prompt Zygmunt's sudden interest in photography? At the time gardening and wine-making were his main outside interests. He started, in black–and–white, using his camera to look at Leeds, not pictorially but perhaps as visual sociology, soon mastering the techniques of developing and printing his own images of the social signs written on the physical sites. Later joining the Leeds Camera Club, he was drawn to portraiture and other classic photography genres – the whole range.

Antony Bryant and Griselda Pollock

The war against forgetfulness (1989)

Zygmunt Bauman
Photographs by Monika Krajewska

> Here the grass is ordinary grass …
> But over the forest
> a flock of Hebrew letters trails

So wrote Polish poet Jerzy Ficowski of the fertile fields and fragrant meadows which have grown over the graves of the largest Jewish community in the history of the Diaspora. Cemeteries are sacred places for Jews; one cannot use the land of the graveyard, nor the grass which grows on it. In the Jewish townships of central and eastern Poland, the pious visited the graves once a year, in the month of Ellul. For the rest of the year grass was allowed to grow freely, wild bushes seeded themselves and, left undisturbed, took the graveyards in their possession. The tangled maze of bramble, thistle, gnarled tree branches and overgrown grasses were like the torn-apart garments of Jewish mourning. The Holocaust came and Ellul ceased to be different from other months. The graveyards stay silent. Lamentations of the living do not disturb the dead. Old gravestones have drowned in triumphant wilderness, sunk into earth, crumbled, vanished. First the visitors died, then the graveyards they visited, then most of those who remembered them.

> Threefold dead of the graveyard:
> Through death,
> Broken tombstone,
> Forgetfulness[1]

'Ashes at the roots of others. Growing grass, growing no memory' – wrote Ficowski in his 'Letter to Marc Chagall'.[2] No memory? But who are the others?

One morning, a decade or so ago, Monika Krajewska set off from her Warsaw home for a long walk through the broken tombstones and for a long war against

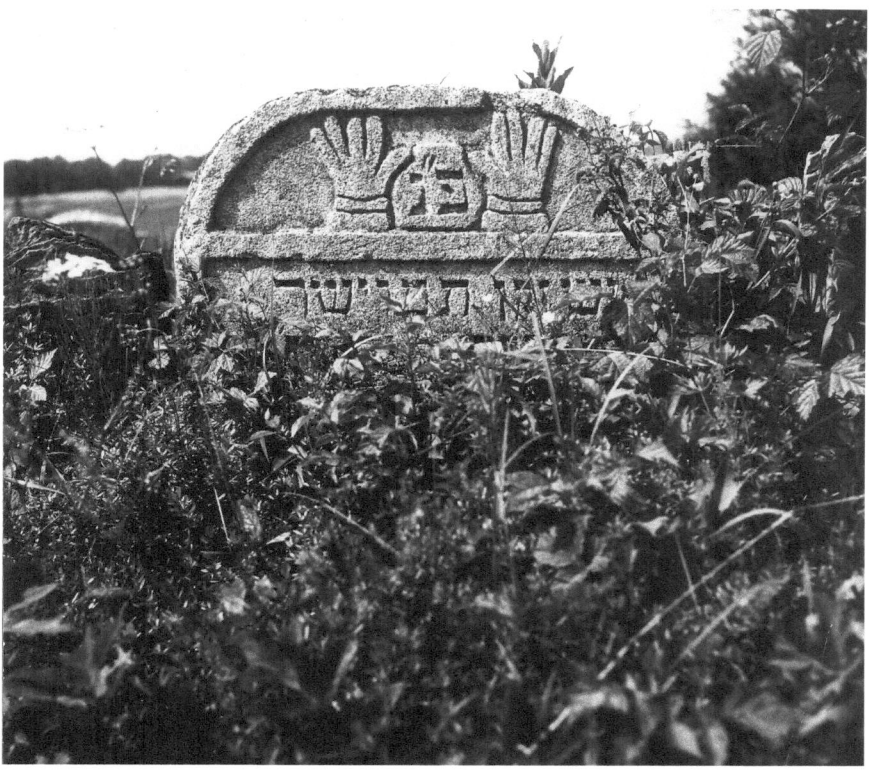

forgetfulness. She took with her an old camera, a few rolls of film and her husband, Stanisław Krajewski. Monika, a language specialist and an editor of art books, came from a Polish Catholic family. Stanisław, a mathematician and now also a theologian and historian of Judaism, descended from a long line of Polish Communists who, with each generation, found it increasingly difficult (and thought it increasingly irrelevant) to distinguish between Jewish origins and Polish identity.

The walk took Monika and Stanisław several years. The couple wandered from one Godforsaken little township to another, along remote bridleways and dust tracks, through peasant fields and small hamlets lost in the woods. Everywhere, they asked the same question: do you remember? The Jews lived here, didn't they? Where did they bury their dead? Surely there must have been a graveyard somewhere around? Please, lead us there. Show us where it was.

Yes, Jews lived there; and those among them who managed to die before Treblinka still lay there, in the woods and under the meadows which once were *Batei Kvaroth* – Houses of the Dead – and now are the only houses of the eight-hundred-year-old community. Sometimes the couple found a graveyard almost complete, miraculously preserved though overgrown and abandoned. Mostly they found solitary tombstones, lost in the midst of a peasant field, protruding from a hillock incongruously rising above the flat meadow, or hidden inside a clump of trees, bafflingly out of place among the vast stretches of farming land. Everywhere, Monika took photographs. Those paper-thin, fragile defences of memory against the winds of time.

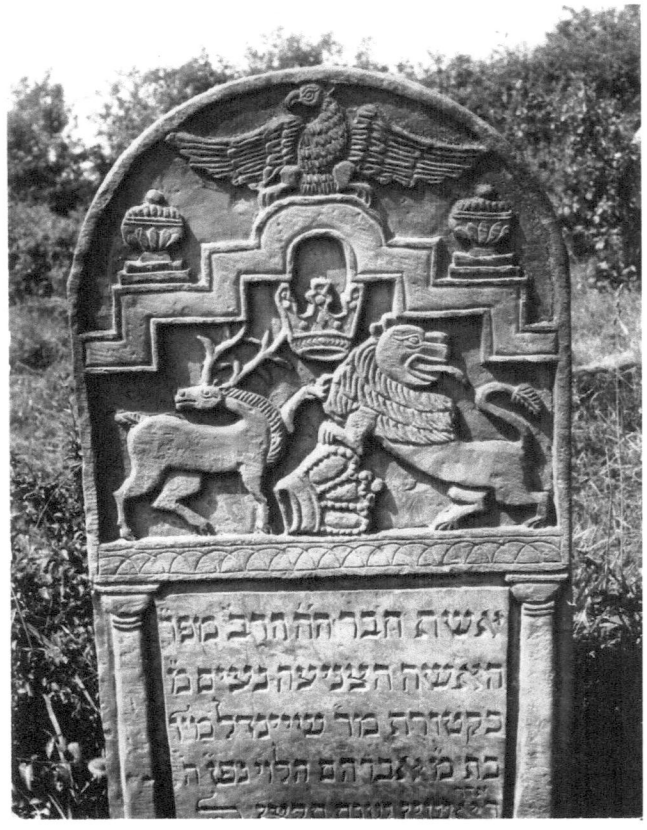

The photographs, introduced by a thoughtful and informative historical essay by Anna Kamienska, made a book.[3] A truly unique book – at the same time a work of art of exquisite beauty, a document of unfathomable value for the historians and a monument to a now extinct, and once culturally rich, intellectually exuberant, three-million-strong nation.

Monika Krajewska is an accomplished photographic artist. She has chosen a haunting object, which made her task deceptively simple and yet in fact excruciatingly difficult. The content could easily dominate the form, emotions could easily overwhelm artistic judgement. That this did not happen is a testimony to Krajewska's art. Image by image, the viewer is treated to an absorbing, yet gentle, play of light and shadow, to the vast yet harmoniously assembled array of black and grey tones, to an immaculately logical, yet startling structure of the frame. One feels drawn into the picture, past the trees, bushes and grazing sheep, along the furrows of the peasant field, behind the scattered remnants of the graveyard fence, straight to the solitary, dignified solemnity of the stone – so much out of place, and yet so much a part of the landscape. One stops only in front of the stone to contemplate the sometimes primitive, sometimes refined, but always immaculately recorded craftsmanship, the petrified imprint of murdered talents, lost imagination and forgotten beliefs.

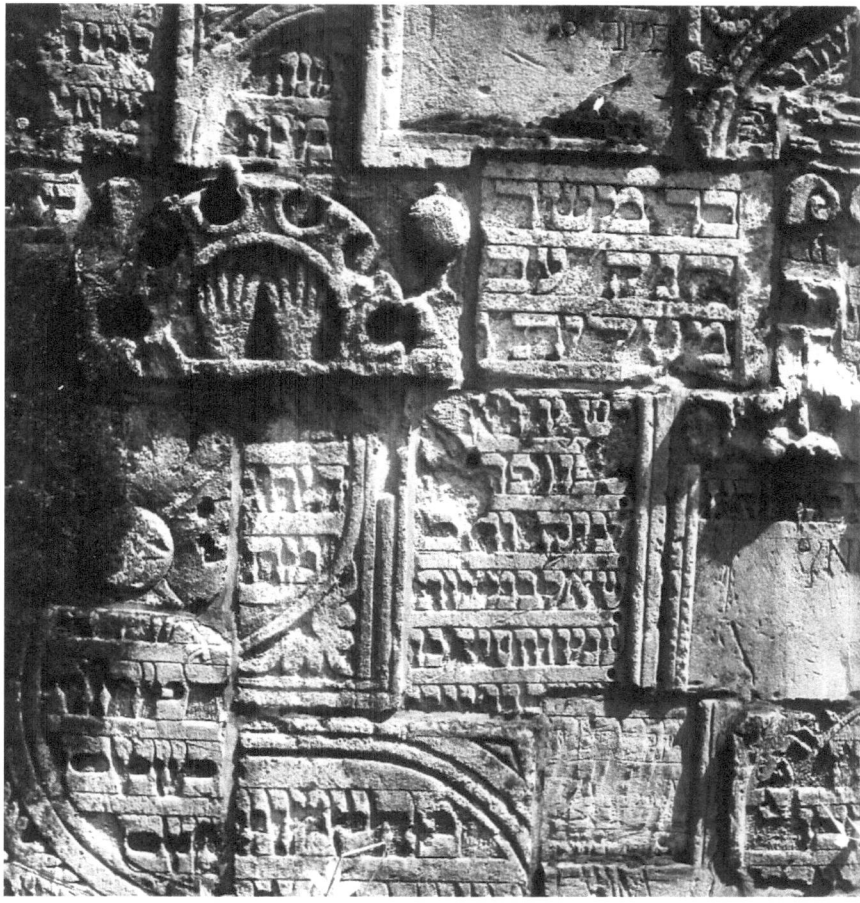

For a historian, Krajewska's photographs are priceless – a document nowhere else to be found. Between themselves they offer a concise history of the beliefs, customs, arts and crafts of the Polish-Jewish community. They testify to the continuity of Jewish tradition and its close kinship with the culture of the host community, to the hold of its inner religious core and its openness to the changing styles of the world. There are gravestones faithful to the Biblical and imported Oriental traditions. There are others which creatively absorbed gothic, baroque, art nouveau, expressionist inspirations. There are stones of austere simplicity and creations of exquisite sculpture art. Above all, there are inscriptions and carved symbols, the little openings into the vast spiritual life of those who lay buried underneath and to the legacy they wished to bequeath to those who would come to read.

For her tiresome, often dangerous toil, Krajewska has been rewarded with quite a few exciting discoveries. The astonishing variety of the local craftsmanship traditions is one of them.

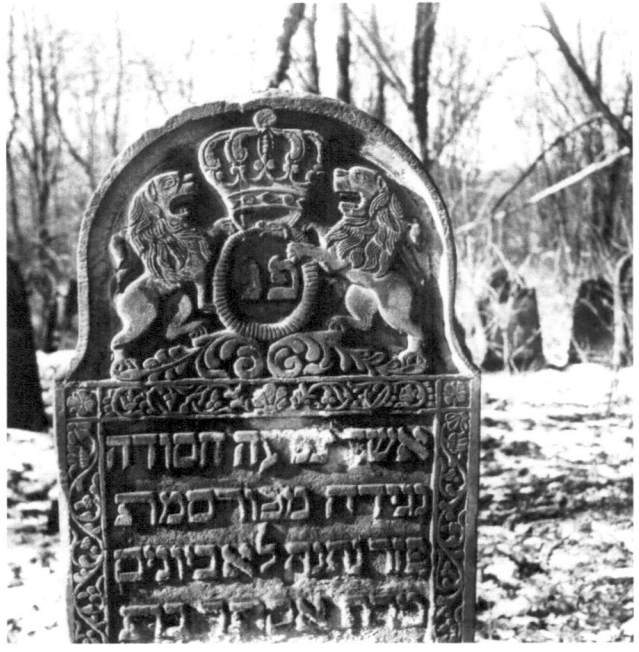

In Lubaczów, for example, folk-style lions appear in a multitude of incarnations from menacingly reptilian to amiably cow-like; in Lesko, nine-branched candelabra are braided like Sabbath *challah*; in Sieniawa, a wealth of symbols is encircled by twining plants and arabesques; and in Tarnów, Mikołów near Katowice, and Mszczonów, master stonecutters attempted a quadrangular [*sic*] stylization of Hebrew letters.[4]

In Poland, a country notorious for its permanent shortage of paper and printing presses, the book was published in an edition of forty thousand copies. It is now an avidly sought bibliographic rarity. Monika Krajewska did not stop her research after the book was published. She has since found more of the forgotten communities and photographed hundreds of monuments of their life and culture. She has also advanced considerably the scholarly analysis of the discovered inscriptions and visual symbols. The new book, now prepared, is certain to raise the achievement of the first to new heights. Outside Poland, though, there seems to be little demand for it.

On a cold and misty November morning (the Catholic Day of Remembrance of the Dead) my wife and I visited the Warsaw Jewish Cemetery at Okopowa Street. At the gate stood luminaries of Polish intellectual life with collection boxes in their hands. We recognised the distinguished historian Professor Gieysztor, an internationally renowned logician and the liberal opposition candidate for the Rectorship of Warsaw University, Professor Szaniawski; Duryasz, the famous actor of the Polish theatre and the contemporary historian Professor Teresa Prekierowa who were among a large and growing group of prominent scholars, artists and journalists. They came to collect money on behalf of the citizenship Committee for the Conservation of the Cemeteries and the Monuments of Jewish Culture in Poland. These intellectuals are perhaps setting a pattern as Andrzej Kuśniewicz, the leading Polish writer, ceded the literary prize awarded by the monthly *Literatura* on behalf of that Committee. Polish passers-by (Okopowa Street leads to Powązki, the largest of Warsaw cemeteries) filled the boxes with coins and banknotes. The only person who studiously looked the other way was an American tourist in the formal garb of a Lubavitch Chassid.

The Polish war against forgetfulness goes on in earnest. There is a genuine popular movement (not to be confused with the government-sponsored public-relations exercises) aimed at the rescuing of Jewish history and culture from oblivion. A movement which draws its zeal from the recognition that that history was part of Polish history and that culture lived intimately close to Polish culture. A movement which wants the physically destroyed nation to live forever in the memory of the nation which stayed alive.

The effort is not entirely disinterested. True, in no small a part it is prompted by an all-too-human sense of duty towards the murdered neighbours. But it has other motives too. It stems from the belief that the long history of Jews in Poland has more to offer to the living than an outlet for the occasional release of excess sentimentality. Polish Jews – by far the largest and the longest-lasting community since the beginning of Jewish dispersal – had a distinguished history as an extraordinarily creative community. They made a highly important contribution to theology, philosophy, literature and moral thought. Their history left a rich heritage, now scattered and buried like the stones of Jewish graves, but waiting to be dug out and repossessed by its rightful descendants. Belatedly, but for strong reasons, the Poles now reclaim their heirloom. They do not seem to have any serious contestants.

Notes

1 Piotr Matywiecki, translated by Rafael Scharf.
2 Translated by Keith Bosley with Krystyna Wandycz.
3 Monika Krajewska, *Czas Kamieni (Time of Stones)* (Warsaw: Interpress, 1982).
4 Monika Krajewska, from the catalogue of exhibition *Traces in the Landscape* at Leventhal-Sidman Jewish Community Center, Newton, Mass, USA (May–June 1987).

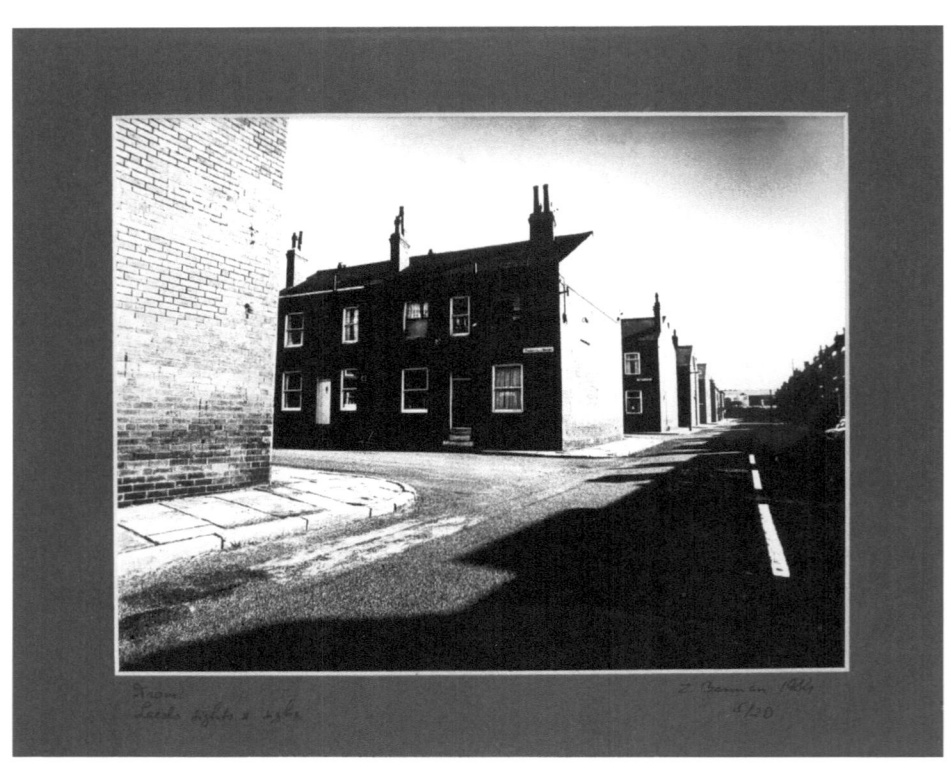

Nearing the end of the long journey I would excitedly search for the familiar landmarks telling me we were almost there: the two golden owls high on a rooftop; the boat on its grassy moor; then finally the iconic university steps, where I would picture *Dziadzia*'s hurried arrival at the department in the early hours, ready to get to work in peace. Then soon after, as though following his journey home, we'd arrive. *Dziadzia* stood on the corner of the road, waiting, *Babcia* patiently inside. Back then, as a child, I didn't know how the last leg of our long journey to my grandparents' house was filled with stories and memories that I was yet to discover.

Years on, as a student at the same University, I found myself following in his footsteps, travelling to and from home – in my case, one of Leeds's many red-brick terraces that had become student accommodation. And so too I began visiting my grandparents, for the first time alone. I remember the nervousness I felt on the first such visit, though this soon gave way to the ritual of being fed and watered beyond any reasonable requirement, and sent off with the customary block of Cheddar cheese (a regular token gift). For years I made *Dziadzia*'s journey, testing my ability to run the distance, cycling in the pouring rain, abandoning my car having unexpectedly drunk too much to drive home. It was during these visits that I heard tale after tale of his journeys during our shared commute through Leeds.

A favourite story was of one of their first outings in Leeds, when *Babcia* requested that they find somewhere for a cup of coffee. *Dziadzia* described driving along what was still at that time a very unfamiliar road until he found the word they were looking for, displayed above a building, tucked around the corner: coffee! Once inside and armed with their – unfortunately mediocre – beverage, they decided to investigate the food on offer, something which they had never tried: fish and chips. Though the arrival of their meal wrapped in a newspaper was the source of much amusement, this, *Dziadzia* would tell me, was the start of his love affair with the great British dish.

In the more recent past, *Dziadzia* decided to take the bus into the city to catch a train. Being so familiar with the route, he timed his journey on the basis of his many years' experience. Unfortunately his early morning commute had somewhat warped his expectation, and he found himself running late. Rather than taking the risk of sitting in heavy traffic he decided, despite being in his late eighties, to get off the bus and run the remaining three miles. Amazingly, he made his train!

That journey, which we shared across decades, was one that I travelled one last time by bus on the rainy morning of 9 January 2017, finally to say goodbye. A journey through time, to this day, alive with memories.

Sofia Hepworth

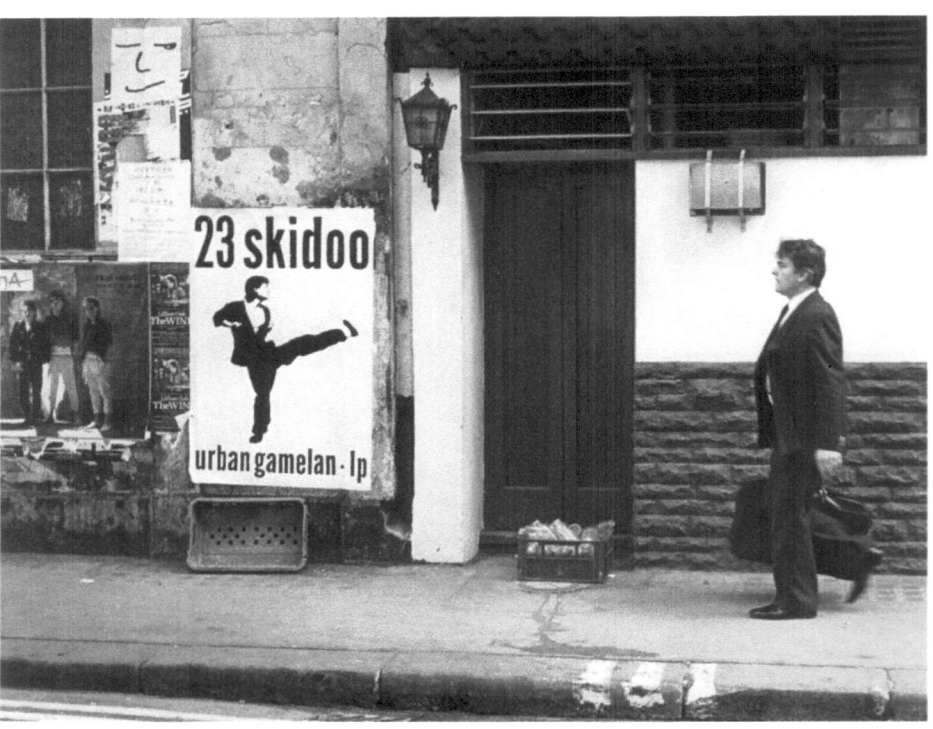

The decisive moment … what Henri Cartier-Bresson meant by this phrase was a fortuitous and spontaneous meeting of visual and psychological elements of a scene; a meeting so fleeting that capturing it necessitates shooting from the hip, a decisive click of the camera shutter. 'To take photographs means to recognise – simultaneously and within a fraction of a second – both the fact itself and the rigorous organisation of visually perceived forms that give it meaning.' Not known for his patience, my father was unlikely to have lain in wait, as so many followers of Bresson did, hoping for a decisive moment to present itself before his camera, like some elusive beast to a wildlife photographer. With his sociologist's eye he would have come to the urban scene knowing what he wanted to capture. But even then, I have a feeling that he was in too much of a hurry to be quite aware of the riches the image he captured contained. Not at the time. Maybe later.

A photograph after all – like a painting – reveals its meaning slowly; much more so than the time it takes to press the shutter. It needs unhurried looking, longer than the 16 seconds the average gallery visitor will allegedly spend in front of any one work of art. Under a patient gaze a painting or a photograph will unravel and offer up its meaning like a flower-bud opening and releasing its scent in the warmth of the sun.

We see an office worker making his daily commute.

Soberly dressed, eyes fixed ahead, his gait mechanical.

He will traverse this space in the opposite direction in eight hours' time.

For this split second he is freeze-framed inside a black-and-white rectangle of a wall: trapped (perhaps the photographer meant to say) in the inescapable certainties of an ordered and predictable life. Nothing of great import ever happens between 9 and 5, as someone once said.

Black-and-white: day followed by night … good day, bad day … peaks and troughs … feast and famine after and before payday … all of which might give one's existence a semblance of variety, but ultimately hold it prisoner to the well-worn habits, tired routines, unquestioned beliefs and low expectations of one who had resigned their grip on hope.

A hopelessness magnified by the realisation, on further examination, that the black-and-white rectangle trapping our insouciant office worker is just one of at least ninety other rectangles in this image, large and small, multiplied even further through any number of combinations. The monotony of an endless procession of days.

But here is another, less obvious message, possibly lost even on this sociologist-photographer, for all his reputed grasp of the cutting edge of culture of every era. He frames his shot as a dialogue with a figure on a nearby poster, engaged in his own (if more exotic) geometry of a martial arts practitioner. He is promoting the 1984 release of an LP by post-punk group *23 Skidoo*. Their tracks, whose meditative gamelan percussion rhythms might seem to echo the photograph's own formalities and the repetitiveness of the office worker's days, nevertheless strain and push against comfort and convention by their combative titles (*Coup, Helicopterz, Fire, Kongo-Do*) and their aggressive vocals and colourful and highly emotive melodies.

A rebellious undercurrent lending, through contrast, an added piquancy to the decisive moment for those with time to stop and contemplate.

Lydia Bauman

Praxis, time, seeing: thoughts on the relationship between Zygmunt Bauman's sociology and his photography

Jack Palmer

Sociologists have produced a great deal of sociological commentary on the discipline, its exemplary figures and its public intellectuals. Typically, when we write commentaries on a social thinker, if they are no longer alive and cannot be consulted themselves, we begin with their already-known ideas as presented in their published works and perhaps, if they are available, lecture transcripts, media appearances and so on. These are then contextualised with reference to the socio-economic, political and cultural processes in which they are embedded and to which they respond. The ideas are often also considered in relation to the specific social position of the thinker in the time and place within which they lived and thought. If we are fortunate, we might be able to draw on a good biography of the thinker for this purpose, perhaps even an autobiography. Luckier still, if we may have access to an archive in which various traces of the imbrications of life and thought are stored for posterity.

We have this archive, in the case of Zygmunt Bauman. I am especially fortunate because I am one of the scholars who helped establish the archive at the University of Leeds. In the process, I have often been struck by the archive's openness to elucidation, even if fragmentarily and elusively, of something that tends to be rarely addressed in sociological commentaries on sociologists, namely the *process of the creation* of knowledge. *How* a particular sociologist worked, as distinct from the 'methods' that they deployed, tends to be neglected completely or to be relegated to the status of biographical detail. Omitted are those everyday *practices* in which intellectuals go about their day-to-day business.[1]

These practices include reading and writing. Zygmunt Bauman's day began at four in the morning, writing beginning after a browse of the morning newspapers, and he tended to read in the afternoons.[2] Mornings were for

production, afternoons for *investment*, as he put it.[3] Among these regular intellectual practices, we might also consider 'interaction rituals', in the sense outlined
in Randall Collins's magisterial *Sociology of Philosophies*, proximate gatherings at
conferences, lectures, seminars and so on.[4] We could also consider practices as
embedded within the daily life of an academic department, the strategising and
jostling for recognition and status among its constituents as addressed by Pierre
Bourdieu in *Homo Academicus*.[5] We might also expand our definition of writing
beyond the production of scholarly works so that it incorporates correspondence.[6] From the archive, we see that he also regularly attended concert halls
and theatres, watched significant amounts of film and television, walked in the
Yorkshire countryside around Leeds, hosted dinner parties and debated with
breakfast guests at his home in Lawnswood Gardens. Overall, we might say
that the promise of the archive for the sociologist of intellectuals is less a chest
of lost treasure which holds some secret key to the work, than a storehouse
of the 'documents of a life' which are the mundane ground in which ideas
germinate.[7]

He was also, of course, a keen photographer. Since it is axiomatic today
to refute the neat separation between life and laboratory even in the natural
sciences, I do not think that Bauman's photography can be cleanly separated
from his sociology, as a hobbyist curio. Bauman's photographic work has some
connection to his sociological work. But what is the nature of this connection? I
do not want to argue that photography assumed a surrogate role for his sociological concerns, that photography was only sociology by another means. The
relationship between photography and sociology in Bauman's oeuvre is not a
simple one. Indeed, at first glance, it is their distinction that is most apparent.
At no point does Bauman's photography cross over into his work. His books
and articles are almost completely textual, the only exceptions being those early
studies in Poland which contain figures and charts of the likes that he would
later come to skewer in his critique of managerial sociology.[8] Photography is
barely discussed in his sociology, in contrast to, say, that of Jean Baudrillard,
Howard Becker and Bourdieu, who sought to understand photography as a
sociological phenomenon.[9] The only explicit work to be published on photography in his lifetime – 'The war against forgetfulness' (pp. 28–34 above) – was
about photographs taken by somebody else, Monika Krajewska.[10]

What is more, practically speaking, his sociology and photography circu-
lated and gestated within very different environments. The ideas contained
in his scholarly writings up until his period of photography – on socialism,
hermeneutics, critical theory, British class history, and politics in Soviet-type
societies – were communicated through elite networks in sociology, in esteemed
departmental seminars, in letterheaded correspondence with international
scholars and in the pages of academic presses and journals. Bauman's practice as

a photographer unfolded in the stubbornly local environs of the Leeds Camera
Club, which he joined in September 1981, in early days referred to in meeting
minutes as 'Prof. Bauman'. The group was based in a few dilapidated rooms in
Stansfeld Chambers in Leeds City Centre. Stansfeld Chambers, minutes of the
club suggest, was often broken into, on several occasions had a leaking roof in
its studio and, at one point, was so hazardous that members discussed raising a
health and safety complaint with the Department of the Environment.[11] And in
contrast to the sombre pages of international academic journals, his exhibitions
were frequented by a public who entered and left freely and whose responses
to his work ranged from highly appreciative to bewildered detachment.

Thought provoking photo's.
Many of a life gone by - never to be repeated
    but by some not forgotten.
Bricked up windows hiding love, laughter &
                        warmth.

Desolate streets crying silent tears.
waiting - waiting like most of us -
    But for WHAT!
                        J.E.B.

A BRILLIANT EXHIBITION!
(this in an opinion of an art critic who
has lived in Leeds for three years, but
has never seen it like this!)

Obviously taken by a tutor of Sociology.
The introductory comments are really
quite class, but the photographs are
a very good effort for an amateur,
generally speaking. There are one or

Few academic reviews could match the Leodensian irreverence of the person who wrote in the visitor book (pictured) for his 1986 exhibition 'Street Messages' that 'this was good but it is not brilliant and I have took better photographs at Bridlington'.

Digging below the surface, however, there are some intriguing crossovers between Bauman's sociology and his photography. Thematically, there are some clear associations between certain strands within his photographs and the themes which found their ways into Bauman's writing. There are the striking portraits – including those of refugees, such as the parents of John Schwarzmantel, discussed by Janet Wolff (pp. 90–1 below) – that recall both his discussions of the social type of the stranger and his sociologisation of Levinas's ethics of the face in key works of the 1990s.[12] His street scenes of post-industrial Leeds in exhibitions like 'Street Messages' were taken when he was preoccupied with the themes of post-industrial urban decline and the emergence of consumer society, and with it 'the new poor'.[13] Just two years after the publication of *Memories of Class*, his first foray into the sociology of postmodernity which would occupy him for over a decade, Bauman provided the photographs for a book written by Alan Wolinski on Osmondthorpe, a deprived inner-city area in East Leeds.[14] As Becker suggested, the photographers' theory about what they are looking at, their understanding of what they are investigating, influences the images.[15] The position of the photographers orients them towards certain subjects, scenes and objects, and in this sense it seems clear that Bauman's sociological imagination and photographic imagination intersected at various points. But there is a more complex story than this.

'Suddenly there is no time'

'Somewhere in Newfoundland: bare and barren rock, no blade of grass in sight. A neat, carefully painted wooden fence cuts it across. What does it divide, and from what?' This line appears in an unpublished mosaic essay composed and written during a visiting position at St John's College, Newfoundland, where Zygmunt and Janina lived for a short time in 1986. Though this is not the precise scene depicted in the adjacent image, it is one of Zygmunt Bauman's photographs from St John's, Newfoundland, kindly shared by Irena Bauman. I do not know what this picture will have meant to its taker. To my untrained eye, it is well composed. It could even be a holiday photo, invoking relaxing walks by the sea, rare for a Leeds-dweller, stuck as it is at the centre of England. A longer look gives way to something more melancholic, evoking the images in W.G. Sebald's *Rings of Saturn*. The harsh cliff-face bears the eons of its formation. Some of it has fallen away, threatening the fragile artifices of the cabins below. The cabins themselves look as if they have been hollowed out. The pier is dilapidated, the tethered small fishing boats are rudimentary and look disused. As the Baumans may well have been aware, contemplating idle fishing vessels on their walks, this was the scene of a crisis of industry. St John's, nestled on the Newfoundland coast and one of the oldest European colonial settlements in North America, had been proximate to one of the most abundant cod stocks in the world, attracting European fleets from the sixteenth century. By 1992, this stock would be declared collapsed and a moratorium placed upon fishing it; some 25,000 fishers and 10,000 more in fishing-related occupations lost their jobs.[16]

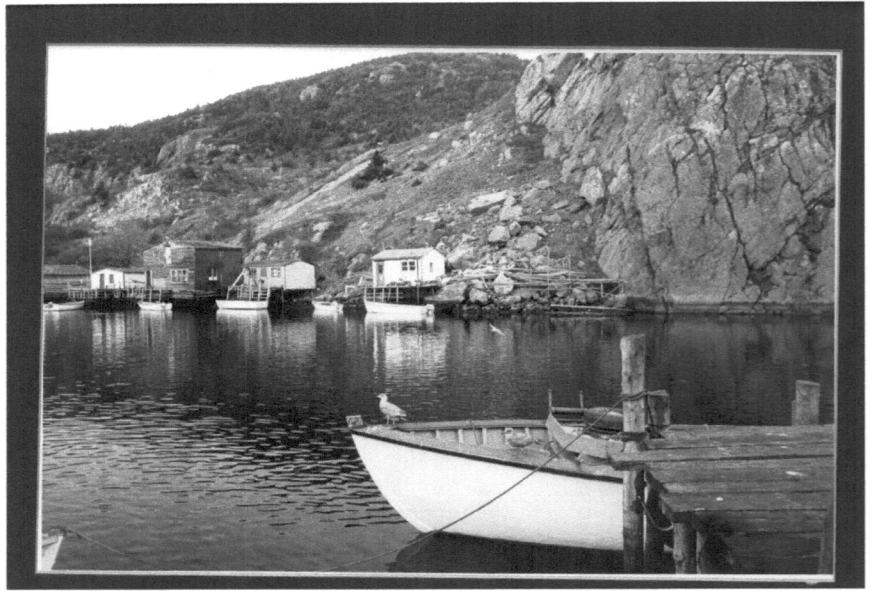

The date of this trip to Newfoundland, and the time of this photograph's taking, coincided with a disillusionment with academia and disciplinary sociology. Indeed, Bauman's intense period of photography unfolded over the most fallow period of his writing career, with a single book, *Memories of Class*, published in 1982 between 1978's *Hermeneutics and Social Science* and 1987's *Legislators and Interpreters*, accompanied by only a handful of essays.[17] It was around this time – experienced by many British leftists as one of deep pessimism and depression at Thatcher's assault on British industry and public institutions – that he unsuccessfully pursued the prospect of early retirement. In June 1987 he wrote to Juan Corradi, one of several US-based intellectuals networked around the new left journal, *Telos*:

> The prospect of five years of the same under Thatcher make one lose interest
> in the future. The few resistant fighters in the universities throw their hands

up – no hope to stop the rot. Ours is not the University I joined seventeen years ago. I do not understand it, I do not like it, I do not fit it. The ultimate irony, of course, that universities are now measured by their 'service to' industry, which – as you know – is in Britain engaged in a disappearing act ... I have quite enough of this – and applied for an early retirement. I do not know whether I'll get it. If I do get it, I'll concentrate on writing – and visiting such places as may wish to invite me (if any). This paradise I would not enter before September 1988 anyway.[18]

This context places the Newfoundland document around November 1986. Part mosaic essay, part collection of aphorisms, it is an extraordinary document. Its form renders it unlike anything else, published or otherwise, in the Bauman canon. It also reveals Newfoundland 1986 as an extremely consequential place and time. Within its pages he writes, among other things, of his responses to Lanzmann's film *Shoah* (which he and Janina would have seen a year earlier) and its message of the 'rationality of evil'. He also reflects on what it means to be an intellectual in exile. There are philosophical musings on death and mortality. It is as if all of the books which appeared in that prolific spurt following the publication of *Legislators and Interpreters* are being set within it. Into the late 1980s and 1990s, publishing works like *Modernity and the Holocaust* and travelling for international speaking engagements as his profile increased (freed up by retirement, in 1991), he appears to have left Leeds Camera Club. Its membership had been declining since Bauman joined, by which time he was recorded in the minutes simply as 'Sigi'. Mirroring trends at clubs across the country, its decline reflected the emergence of trade processing of colour photographs and the popularity of the disposable camera.[19] Leeds Camera Club disbanded in 1994, after reaching its centenary in the previous year.

The Newfoundland essay also reveals that Zygmunt was preoccupied with time and its passing. When I found a copy of the first page of the document on an Amstrad file (both Janina and Zygmunt used an Amstrad machine in the 1980s), it bore the title 'Before it is too late'. The first line of the manuscript (pictured) is 'suddenly, there is no time'. It was written in November, the month of his birthday and in which he often penned his most personal offerings. I am told by Anna Sfard that November was a time of 'stocktaking' – the idea of *This Is Not a Diary* was conceived in November, and his memoir *The Poles, the Jews and I* was also started in November. Its year is 1986, meaning it would have been written around his sixty-first birthday, an age at which, according to the aforementioned Sebald, many exiles become preoccupied with their own past – although for Bauman, as for Sebald, the confrontation with the past did not and could not salve the condition of exile of its liminality.[20]

His photography was also motivated in some part by this preoccupation with time. As is documented in 'Thinking Photographically', a short piece

St John's, November 1986

'Suddenly, there is no time...'

This is how I feel. Or, rather, this is how I report what I feel, make my feeling known to myself.

'Suddenly, there is no time...' Silly remark, to think of it. Can one have time the way ~~ixixx~~ one has Bread? Or money? Or home?

But perhaps one can have time the same way one has the will to do things, to love, to endure. So perhaps the remark is not that silly, after all.

What makes it silly is the habit of thinking of 'having time' the same way one thinks of 'having bread'. 'Having bread' matters. 'Having' time as if one had bread, does not. Or, rather, time had in such a way does not matter.

Wisdom of English: the idioms 'Ihave no time for...', and 'I do not care for...', are synonymous.

So now I have explained it to myself. I understand. I know. And yet...

'Suddenly, there is no time...' feels very much like 'suddenly, there is no bread'. Nothing to do with will. Or, rather, the will has reached the wall it cannot any more bite its way through. Even if it dreams ahead of itself; even if it measures its strength by the voracity of its ambitions.

Finally, 'having time' has become exactly like 'having bread'. Comparison is not silly any more. What makes it true is the old age.

To be old (to know it) means: time is had the same way the bread is.

The only certain certainty is death. Is the lust for certainty the work of Thanatos? Is the cynicism of the Old, Libido's last stand?

'Do not kill yourself!' – ~~I am~~ warned. If you smoke, you are killing yourself. If you eat fat, you are killing yourself. If you are getting fat, you are killing your self even more.

And what if I do not? Who is killing me then?

on photography which I edited and gathered from the fragments contained within the archive, in various letters to photographic journals and exhibition catalogues, he saw photography as 'a technique of cleansing experience from the decomposing solvent of time', which 'may freeze and thus make available to our reflection the apparently trivial happenings, too brief to be noticed as they occur – often even by the actors themselves'.[21] In 'The War against Forgetfulness', photographs are characterised as 'paper-thin, fragile defences of memory against the winds of time'.[22] The Newfoundland photograph is a curious artefact, then. It preserves in the flux of time a happy and intellectually stimulating time with Janina on another continent, but it also precipitates the most productive and significant period of his sociology and heralds, therefore, a departure from photography itself.

'Always a window, never an eye'

Anna Zeidler-Janiszewska, who died in the same year as Zygmunt Bauman, coaxed out of him one of the very few public discussions of his photography in their dialogue book, *Życie w kontekstach* (*Life in Contexts*).[23] It was in these pages in 2007 that he revealed a certain practical appeal in photography:

> In photography, I was fascinated by the magic of a darkroom. I discovered the relativity of an image, relativity of representation, relativity of interpretation – by obtaining several distinct images with diverse themes, diverse 'built in' interpretation – from one single negative, and such difference was triggered by sheer movement of the palm between the lens and the photo paper, by framing, by changing the chemical composition of developers and fixers.[24]

His passion for photography had long cooled before the dawn of the digital age, which with its central motif, disposability, must have seemed distasteful to somebody whose biggest gripe with consumer society was its waste (of human lives, of consumer products, of planetary resources).[25] In one of his attendances at the annual general meeting of the Leeds Camera Club, he also lamented the emergence of trade processing of colour photographs, noted to have commented that 'photography was a craft hobby and that work produced should be the photographer's own from start to finish'.[26]

To Zeidler-Janiszewska he also admitted that 'I think that I searched for answers to my questions in photography, in the same way as in my academic work, being unable to express in words what can be expressed by images'.[27] I am intrigued by this evocation of the relationship between words and images. But I am less interested by the boundaries between them in Bauman's work, where words fail and images take over and vice versa, than in their interrelations. I have suggested that Bauman's sociological imagination had a sensitising effect on his photographic practice. A more complicated case can be made, I suggest, for a feedback effect, his photographic practice in turn informing a particular expression of his sociological imagination.

Bauman, as I have said, never literally mixed his sociology and his photography. He cannot therefore be assimilated into the canon of 'visual sociology', be placed alongside practitioners of the 'photo-essay', and it does not seem that (as with Sebald, for example) there was a symbiotic relationship between specific photographs and pieces of writing, the photographs thus forming an intrinsic part of the writing process. That said, one can delineate a *visual turn* in Bauman's sociology that is coeval with his turn to photography in the late 1970s. He himself came to recognise, in an interview in 2011, that 'the visual does seem to be the most thoroughly grasped and recorded among my impressions and "seeing" supplies the key metaphors for reporting the perception'.[28] But it was not always the case. To put it physically, the sense organ at the forefront of his works of the 1970s in the Leeds period might be said to be the ear and its corollary, the larynx, with its capacity to produce the sensation of spoken sound, the basis of human communication.[29]

Something changes into the better-known work of the 1980s. He becomes interested in the social and moral aspects of seeing – the sight of the face of the Other in their proximity, or the visibility of suffering and the varied social mechanisms which render it invisible. Visuality also permeates his analyses of political modernity, such as in *Memories of Class*, published a year after he joined Leeds Camera Club. The modern state, he argued, rendered populations visible through statistical counting and demographic mapping for the purposes of intervention and order-building, with Bentham's panopticon – that invention for seeing-all – as the paradigm. It warrants a mention that Bauman wrote an endorsement for the cover of Yale anthropologist James C. Scott's *Seeing Like a State*.[30] Later, in *Legislators and Interpreters*, there is the 'gardening state' which embodies the tendency to see the social world as a potential wilderness in need of taming.

It is at this point that metaphor permeates his writings, which in his sociology is an appeal to visuality, to seeing things differently or in a new light. Metaphors play a dual role in Bauman's sociology. Firstly, he elucidates how solidified or familiarised concepts – that of 'assimilation', for example, in *Modernity and Ambivalence*, 'culture' in *Legislators and Interpreters* and 'class' in *Memories of Class* – have their provenance in metaphor, and how their appropriation reveals the working of power-laden social processes. He names this task *defamiliarisation*, an attempt to unravel what Hans Blumenberg termed the 'complex field of transitions from metaphors to concepts', wherein the metaphor is 'absorbed by the word'.[31] The second role of metaphor is to provide a more adequate language for capturing societal shifts, *familiarising* them. Hannah Arendt is also an important source of inspiration for Bauman at this point. What she termed 'metaphorical thinking' was a practice of *seeing similars in dissimilars*.[32] Her discussions of metaphor in her unfinished *Life of the Mind* are shot through with appeals to visuality and sight. The metaphor consists in 'bridging the abyss between inward and *invisible* mental activities and the world of *appearances*'. Metaphors 'serve as models to give us our bearings *lest we stagger blindly among experiences* that our bodily senses with their relative certainty of knowledge cannot guide us through'.[33]

These sorts of connections between the thinker and the public in the 'space of appearances' can be made in Bauman's short and fragmented, though extremely rich, reflections on photography. Photography, he reflected, 'may only hope to be a window; never an eye'.[34] In other words, photography should not proscribe but opens up a world to its viewer, an invitation to explore it. Here, the reader must be reminded of how the Holocaust, as he encountered it as a reader of Janina's *Winter in the Morning*, famously became a *window* for Bauman, displacing the image of a sealed and neatly delineated picture-frame. As a window, it points beyond itself, opening out on to the dark potential of modernity. It is also striking that we find that Bauman understood photography in terms that recall his well-known dictum that sociology ought to aspire towards 'defamiliarizing the familiar':

> In our daily bustle, we rarely have time, or strength, or will to stop, to look around, to think. We pass by things giving them no chance to puzzle, baffle or just amuse. Photography may make up for our daily neglect. It may sharpen our eyesight, bring into focus things previously unnoticed, transform our experiences into knowledge.[35]

Thinking Sociologically (2001), likewise, is effectively tantamount to the adoption of an unfamiliar way of seeing as well as a distantiation from inherited, 'common-sense' imaginative frameworks:

> One could say that the main service the art of thinking sociologically may render to each and every one of us is to make us more *sensitive*; it may sharpen up our senses, open our eyes wider so that we can explore human conditions which thus far had remained all but invisible.[36]

'Tell me what is your praxis, and I'll tell you what your world is'

A clue to understanding the kind of symbiosis between sociology and photography that I'm trying to make a case for here can be found in Bauman's own cultural sociology. *Sketches in the Theory of Culture*, Bauman's 'lost book', seized upon exile in 1968, begins with a reference to the 'eternal praxeomorphism of the human way of seeing the world', praxeomorphism defined as the way in which 'people imagine the world in the way they've learned to model it'.[37] This curious concept – his own coinage – evokes *Culture as Praxis*, where he elaborated on the notion that culture consists of a permanent, processual practice of human *ordering* of the world, the continual attempt at generating solidity and certainty in a fundamentally uncertain environment. 'Praxeomorphism' returns in later discussion of Jean Baudrillard, himself a photographer who wrote at length on photography. As he put it: 'it has been said that our perception of the world is incurably anthropomorphic. Wrong. It is *praxeomorphic*.' He continues:

We know of the world in as far as we act upon it. The knowable world is what we do something about. And the knowledge of the world is the knowledge of what can be done, of what we are capable of doing. We make sense of the world in terms of our sensible (because purposeful) practices. In the age of mechanics, the nervous system appeared to Descartes or La Mettrie as a neat contraption of valves, gears, strings and fluids. This vision was later replaced by one of an electrical grid and transmission of impulses. Later still, in the age of the radar, intelligence was deciphered as the scanning of the space of possibilities. Now we see the brain as a computer, and what we see follows faithfully the capacities of successive computer generations. *Tell me what is your praxis, and I'll tell you what your world is.*[38]

Is it so surprising, then, that his *praxis* as a photographer – honed in the Leeds Camera Club and moulded into a way of seeing in the world, defamiliarising everyday existence through the camera lens and freezing in form those transient moments in the liquidity of time – crossed over in the various ways that I have depicted into the *world* that he depicted in his sociology?

Notes

1 Charles Camic, Neil Gross and Michelle Lamont, 'Introduction: The Study of Social Knowledge Making', in *Social Knowledge in the Making* (Chicago: University of Chicago Press, 2011), 1–40.

2 Aleksandra Kania, 'Living with Zygmunt Bauman, Before and After', *Thesis Eleven*, 149.1 (2018), 88.

3 Zygmunt Bauman, *Making the Familiar Unfamiliar: Conversations with Peter Haffner* (Cambridge: Polity, 2020), 42.

4 Randall Collins, *The Sociology of Philosophies: A Global History of Intellectual Change* (Cambridge, MA: Harvard University Press, 1998).

5 Pierre Bourdieu, *Homo Academicus* (Oxford: Blackwell, 1988).

6 Peter Beilharz, *Intimacy in Postmodern Times: A Friendship with Zygmunt Bauman* (Manchester: Manchester University Press, 2020).

7 Ken Plummer, *Documents of Life 2: An Invitation to Critical Humanism* (London: Sage, 2001).

8 See, for example, Zygmunt Bauman, 'Social Structure of the Party Organization in Industrial Works'. *Polish Sociological Bulletin*, 3–4 (1962), 50–64.

9 Jean Baudrillard, *Car l'illusion ne s'oppose pas à la réalité: Photographies* (Paris: Descartes, 1998); Howard Becker, 'Photography and Sociology', *Studies in Visual Communication*, 1.1 (1974), 3–26; Pierre Bourdieu, *Photography: A Middlebrow Art*, trans. Shaun Whiteside (Stanford: Stanford University Press, 1990 [1965]).

10 Zygmunt Bauman, 'The War against Forgetfulness', *Jewish Quarterly*, 36.1 (1989), 44–7. Reprinted pp. 28–34 above.

11 In 1987 minutes of Annual General Meeting. Leeds Camera Club records, West Yorkshire Archive Service, Leeds, WYL1612/1/13. The building, Grade II listed

since 1976, now houses the Carriageworks Theatre and lucrative retail space, its transformation mirroring Leeds's consumerist boom.

12 See *Modernity and Ambivalence* (Cambridge: Polity, 1991) and *Postmodern Ethics* (Oxford: Blackwell).

13 See *Memories of Class: The Prehistory and Afterlife of Class* (London: Routledge & Kegan Paul, 1982) and *Work, Consumerism and the New Poor* (Milton Keynes: Open University Press, 1998).

14 Alan Wolinski, *Osmondthorpe: The Area that Time Forgot. A Study of Community Work on an Inter-war Council Estate* (Hertford: Dr Barnardo's, 1984).

15 Becker, 'Photography and Sociology', 11.

16 David Ralph Matthews, 'Commons versus Open Access: The Collapse of Canada's East Coast Fishery', *The Ecologist*, 25.2–3 (1995), 86.

17 For a more-or-less complete record of Bauman's publications, see the 'living bibliography' on the Bauman Institute website, which I have helped to collate: https://baumaninstitute.leeds.ac.uk/bauman-archive/living-bibliography/.

18 Letter from Zygmunt Bauman to Juan Corradi, 29 June 1987. In Papers of Janina and Zygmunt Bauman, MS 2067/B/5/2.

19 Fujifilm developed and released the currently familiar form of disposable camera in 1986.

20 As Sebald said of the central character in *Austerlitz*: 'Austerlitz himself, as an adult, then conspired, as it were against his own will, in this erasing of his own identity and constructed in his mind a system of avoidance which allowed him to ignore that which constantly troubled him. But as he drew towards retirement age, as so often happens, he felt obliged to confront this problem, and he goes in search, as someone aged around 60, of his own identity.' Quoted in Richard Sheppard, 'Three Encounters with W.G. Sebald (February 1992 – July 2013)', *Journal of European Studies*, 44.4 (2014), 394.

21 Zygmunt Bauman, 'Thinking Photographically', in *Culture and Art: Selected Writings, Volume 1*, ed. Dariusz Brzeziński, Mark Davis, Jack Palmer and Thomas Campbell (Cambridge: Polity, 2021 [1983–1985]), 106.

22 Bauman, 'The War against Forgetfulness', 45 (p. 30 above).

23 Also with R. Kubicki, *Życie w kontekstach. Rozmowy o tym, co za nami i o tym, co przed nami (Life in Contexts: Conversations about What Lies Behind Us and What Lies Ahead of Us)* (Warsaw: WAiP, 2007).

24 Quoted from Anna Zeidler-Janiszewska, 'Zygmunt Bauman's Images'. In Papers of Janina and Zygmunt Bauman, digital file, USB 17, 'AZJ_Zygmunt_Bauman'.

25 See Zygmunt Bauman, *Wasted Lives: Modernity and Its Outcasts* (Cambridge: Polity, 2004).

26 Minutes of the Annual General Meeting of the Leeds Camera Club, 25 February 1986. In records of Leeds Camera Club, WYL1612/1/13.

27 Quoted in Anna Zeidler-Janiszewska, 'Zygmunt Bauman's Images'.

28 Simon Dawes, 'The Role of the Intellectual in Liquid Modernity: An Interview with Zygmunt Bauman', *Theory, Culture & Society*, 28.3 (2011), 131.

29 See, for example, Habermas-influenced discussions *Towards a Critical Sociology: An Essay on Commonsense and Emancipation* (London: Routledge & Kegan Paul, 1976) and *Hermeneutics and Social Science: Approaches to Understanding* (London: Hutchinson and Co., 1978).

30 James C. Scott, *Seeing Like a State: How Certain Schemes to Improve the Human Condition Have Failed* (New Haven: Yale University Press, 1998).

31 Hans Blumenberg, *Paradigms for a Metaphorology*, trans. R. Savage (Ithaca: Cornell University Press, 2010), 81.

32 Bryan Cheyette, *Diasporas of the Mind: Jewish and Postcolonial Writing and the Nightmare of History* (New Haven: Yale University Press, 2013), 8.

33 Hannah Arendt, *The Life of the Mind* (New York: Harcourt Brace Jovanovich, 1978), vol. 1, 104, 109.

34 Bauman, 'Thinking Photographically', 111.

35 Bauman, 'Thinking Photographically', 106.

36 Zygmunt Bauman, *Thinking Sociologically* (Oxford: Blackwell, 1990), 16.

37 Zygmunt Bauman, *Sketches in the Theory of Culture* (Cambridge: Polity, 2018 [1968]), 7.

38 Zygmunt Bauman, 'The Second Disenchantment'. *Theory, Culture & Society*, 4 (1988), 738 (my emphasis).

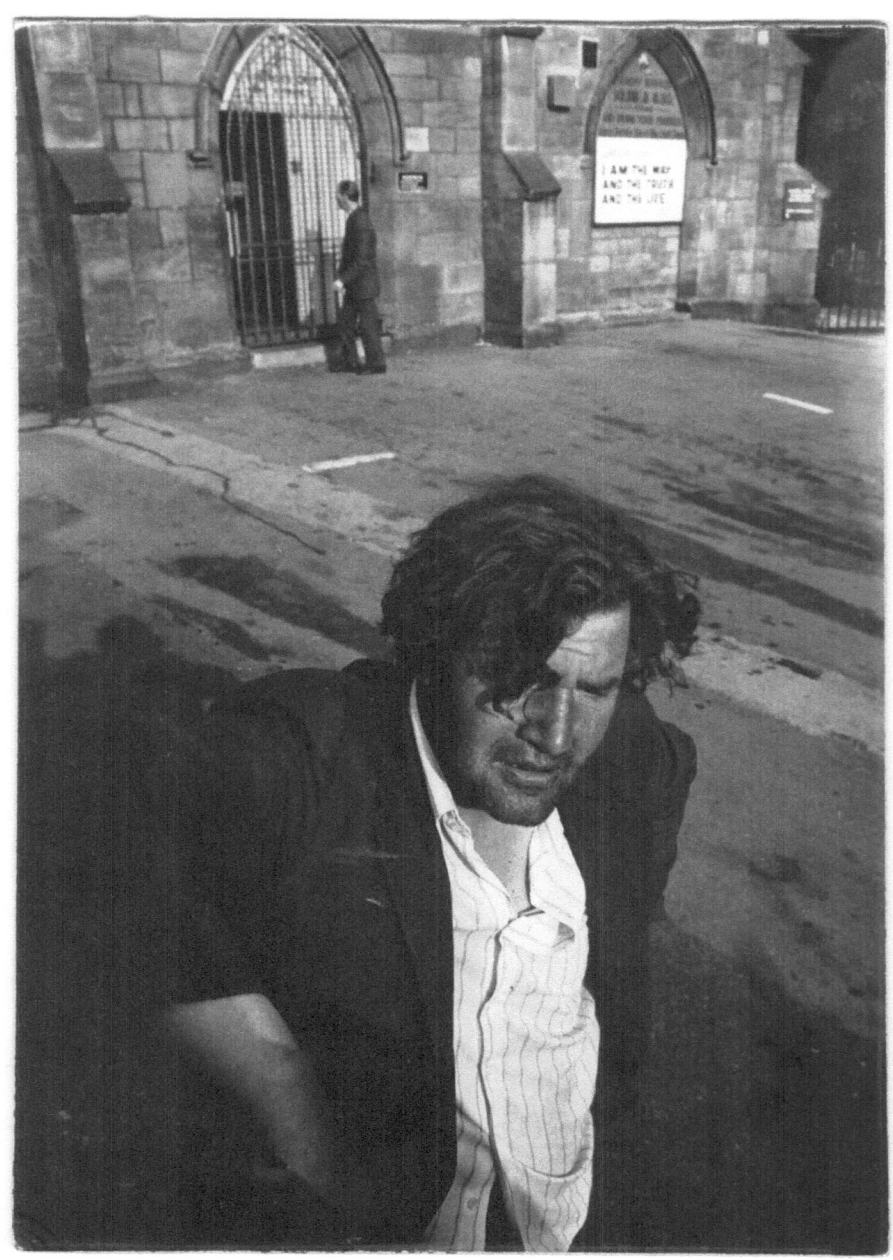

Who is this guy? A man to be afraid of, or one who has been wronged? Victim or perpetrator, or both? Angry, or lost, in despair? A lost soul in the churchyard, or caught by it, frozen in a moment of time?

He does not seem to be homeless; or, at least, he is well dressed. Hair styled? A touch of suave? Shirt tails out, three-day growth, dishevelled, coming off a bender? Jacket sleeve elevated, as was the fashion then, in the 1980s. Remember *Miami Vice*? Not so slick, no pastels, no Don Johnson this. Sick? Alienated? Exasperated? Manic depression, that frustrating mess?

Our photographer employs the period critical device of irony, or juxtaposition. The church's weekly banner announces imminent salvation. Could he be the unwanted arrival, the next preacher? The message is clear: I Am The Way, I Am The Light etc. But salvation is off-centre, too far away. The dominant figure is balanced by another, a turnkey, or minder, who goes about his business, the business of minding rather than salvation. The church is closed. The light is bright; our subject blinks, or his eyes are hooded in reaction. The asphalt is moist. The angle of the camera seems somehow to be elevated.

It's a close-up, staged and framed by its moment. How did Bauman capture this image? Close-up may also mean danger, or at least mutual vulnerability. The photographer violates the space of the subject, risks his humiliation in capturing him down and out, inelegant, indisposed, out of control even if just for the moment. They dance, or perhaps they spin like boxers, for that moment, held together, but wary of the glancing blow or knockout. Street photographers need to know how to run.

The gift of the study is in its sense of the uncanny, its indeterminacy. There is something going on here, but we have no clear idea of what it is. This photograph is not posed, or composed. It carries the atmosphere of the 1980s, early Thatcher, and it conveys some sense of anxiety, of uncertainty. It conveys a mood, but not a message. Its purpose is not enlightenment, so much as to hang an imaginary question mark over the image and the world it emerges out of. This was, after all, Bauman's purpose in photography, as in sociology – not to answer questions, but to help pose them. Like a child looking into a kaleidoscope for the first time, the result is intriguing and disorienting at the same time. Such was his purpose, as best we know: to affirm humanity, to contemplate, or to look into the abyss, and to wonder if we might be capable of better looking after each other.

Peter Beilharz

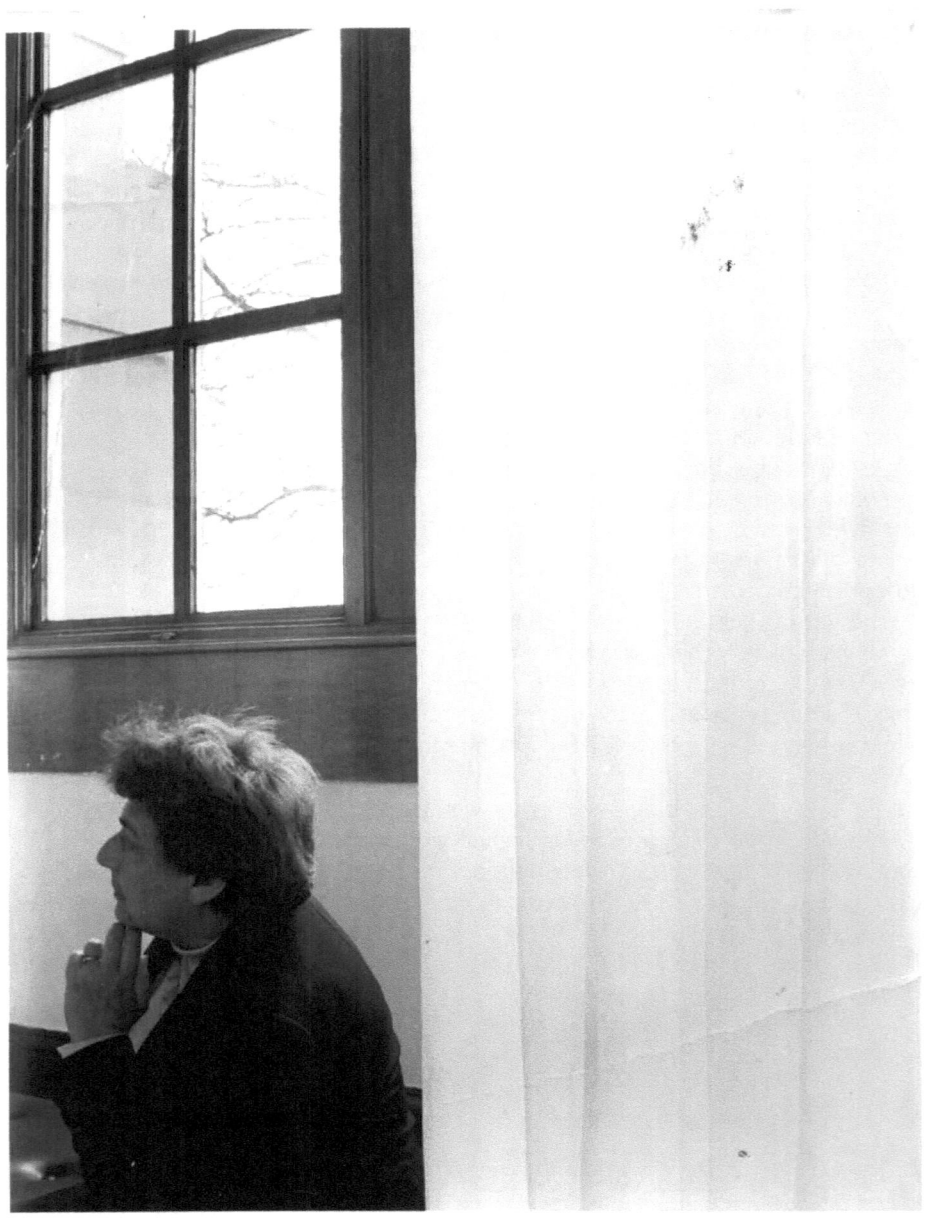

When I was about twelve, we came from Israel to Leeds, to visit *Saba* and *Sabta*, my grandparents. I spent much of the visit alone, wandering around their dim mysterious home, with wild vegetation covering its windows. Piles upon piles of books filled the rooms and heaps of interesting artefacts were scattered all over the place. *Saba*'s photographs accompanied you up the stairs and *Sabta*'s beautiful ceramic pots were scattered on the shelves.

On one of my research trips around the house I came across a framed postcard that hung in the hallway near *Saba*'s study. It was Dali's painting of Jesus on a cross. As I examined the intriguing scene in front of me, I heard *Saba* behind me.

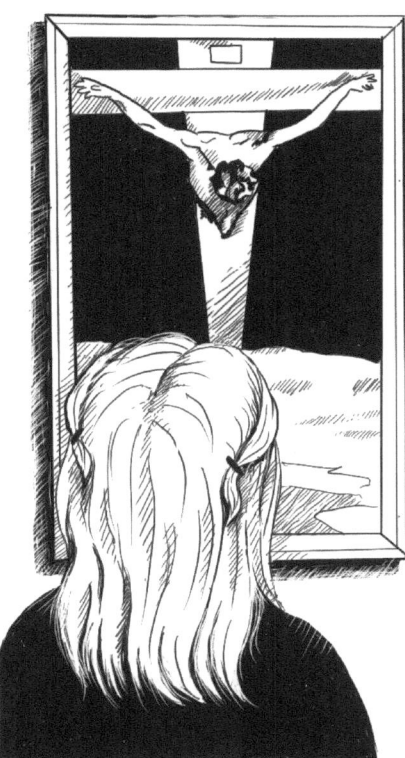

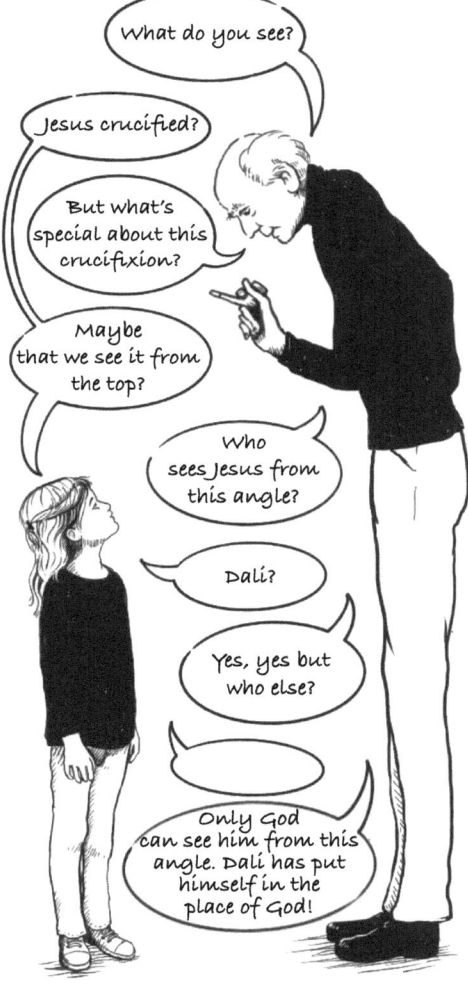

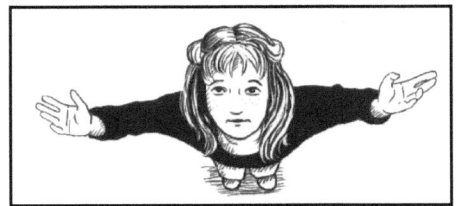

It was then that I became aware of the artists' presence in their own work. Ever since that event, whenever I inspect an artwork sharing the artist's point of view, I make sure to look also at the artist herself.

And thus, when I stood in my grandparents' kitchen in front of this portrait, I saw *Saba* watching *Sabta* staring at the unknown. This reminded me of two paintings: Paul Klee's *Angel of History* (1920) and René Magritte's *Not to Be Reproduced* (1937).

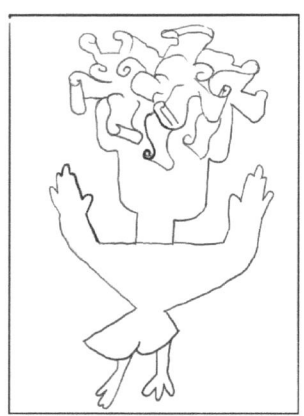

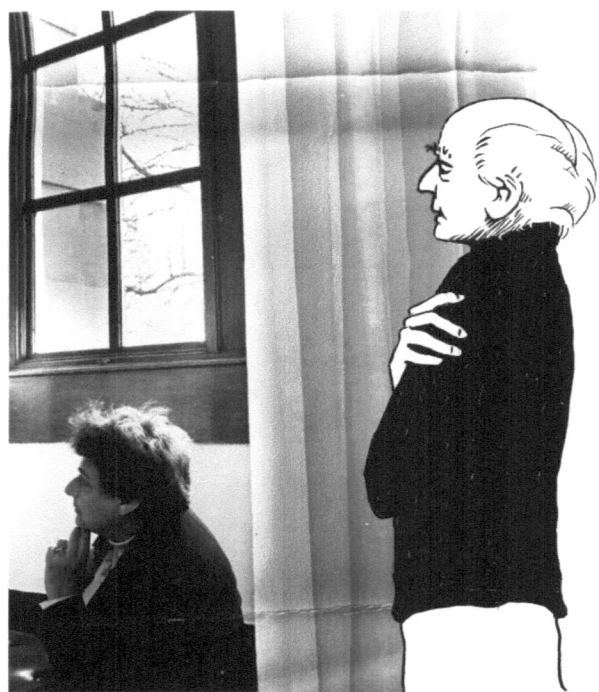

Paraphrasing Walter Benjamin, *Saba* wrote in his last book, *Retrotopia*, that the angel is actually changing his point of view from the past to the future, and is thus caught in limbo between the past and the future. In *Saba*'s photograph, *Sabta* is with her back to us, her pensive gaze directed out of the frame. What is she thinking about? The past or the future? *Saba* depicted her well. In life, just as in the photo, *Sabta*'s thoughts are outside the frame. And so were *Saba*'s. What they thought could only be found in the books they wrote. If at all.

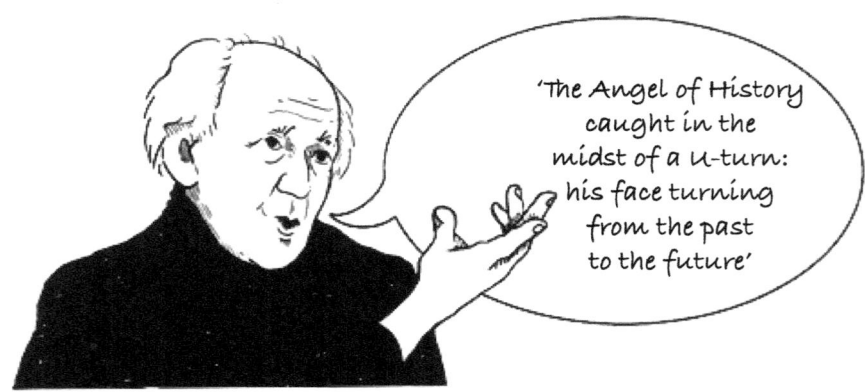

'The Angel of History caught in the midst of a U-turn: his face turning from the past to the future'

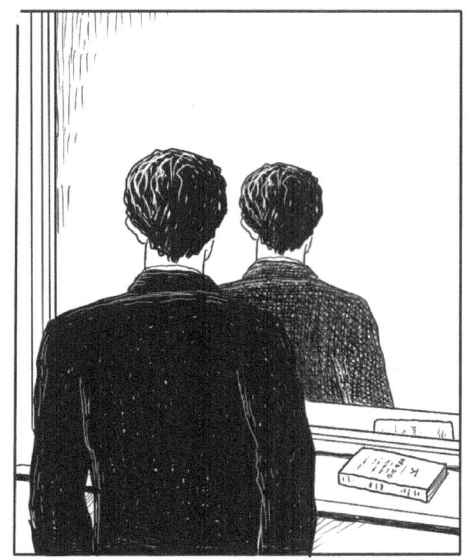

Magritte often dealt with concealment. He believed that the things we see hide the thing that, in fact, we want to see. There is a much concealment in the portrait. The curtain fills more than half the composition; one can hardly see *Sabta*'s face. The movement of *Sabta*'s hand appears staged, but I may be perceiving it in this way because I remember being directed by *Saba* when I modelled for him. There is something romantic about

Saba peeking over *Sabta*'s shoulder. I look at her together with him and wonder what he thinks of her. Does he see her as a reflection of himself? In many ways I did see them as one unit.

Maybe *Saba* wouldn't have agreed with my analysis of the photo. But hey, truth is in the eye of the beholder.

Emi Sfard

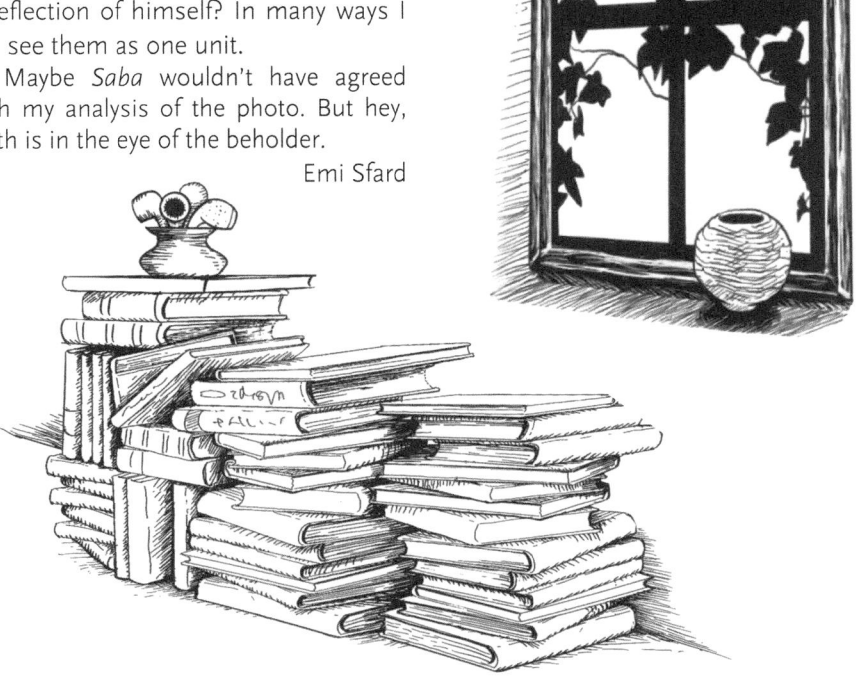

Captured by Zygmunt

Janet Wolff

Janina writes:

> Saturdays are for country walks. We set off at dawn and after a few miles
> drive, leave our car behind and go off into the wild. The open space welcomes
> us to the rising day, the freshening breeze, the morning dew. We plunge into
> the deep silence broken only by birdsong and the peaceful bleating of sheep.
> Walking fast – Konrad first, alert, his camera ready, me far behind and deep
> in my thoughts – we talk very little, but we are together … We pass walls
> of dark Yorkshire stone, laid skilfully without mortar, that after hundreds
> of years are still holding fast and forming a patchwork design on this fertile
> land.[1]

Konrad is her name for Zygmunt in her second memoir. Many years after
these walks, a week after Zygmunt's death, a small group of family and friends
gathered for lunch one last time at Lawnswood Gardens, and Zygmunt's and
Janina's daughters invited me to choose one of his photos. So I have on my desk
now this beautiful little photo of a Yorkshire mill.

For about fifteen years, after I joined Zygmunt in Leeds in 1973, I regularly
drove past the marker at the top of the M62 between Manchester and Leeds – a
stone with a red rose on one side, white rose on the other – symbolising my two
county allegiances.[2] Eventually, and after forty years away, I have ended up
back with the red rose of Lancashire. But my Yorkshire years figure strongly in
my memory, and most especially my time with Zygmunt and Janina.

We kept in touch after I left Leeds in 1988, and in July 2016, just a few
months before his death, I was surprised to receive an email from Zygmunt,
asking if I would consider working on a dialogue book on culture with him. He
had in mind, he said, 'a conversation addressed not to fellow academics, but
to culture's practitioners and cultural practices' objects'. I felt honoured by his
invitation, though I also had serious reservations. I honestly didn't think that in

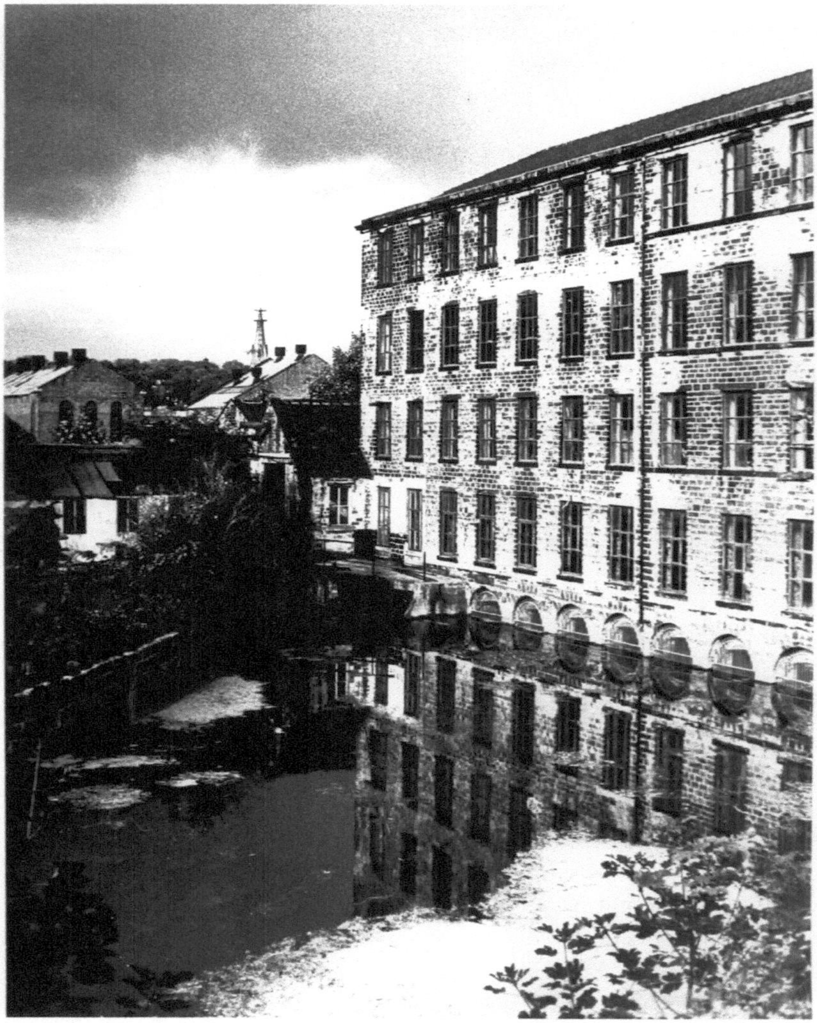

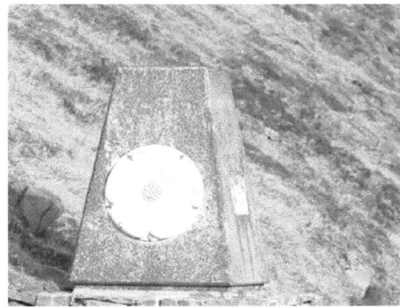

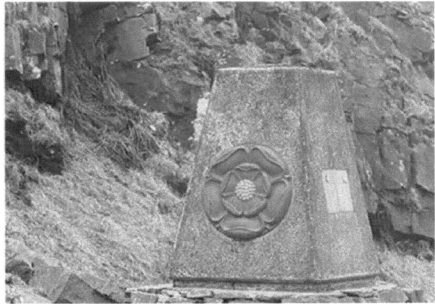

my part of the dialogue I could match his erudition (no question about that), and I don't think he intended me simply to be a neutral interlocutor. In any case, we agreed to continue to think (and email) about it. But he became more ill in the following months, and the conversation in print never happened.

It would have been an unusual volume in one respect – so much of the literature on Zygmunt's work, and almost all of his later dialogue books, are by and with men.[3] Perhaps more interestingly, now that we are thinking about his photographic legacy, I wonder if it would have turned out to be a nice opportunity to explore more his interest in the visual arts. His passion for literature and film is well documented, and indeed one of the late dialogue books is specifically about the relationship between sociology and literature, where he makes the strong case that the two are 'sisters', indispensable to one another.[4] Scattered through his writing over the decades one finds enthusiasm for, or at least reference to, particular artists. Magritte figures large here, and he also wrote a little about others – Calder, Damien Hirst, the Polish artist Joanna Przbyła.[5] And included in the present volume (pp. 28–34 above) is a rare essay by Zygmunt about photography, on the photographs of Monika Krajewska. The editors of a recent volume of Bauman's writings on culture and art quote him:

> I'm interested in art for as long as I remember. I was fascinated primarily by visual art. It is related to music and poetry, which differ from visual arts, in my opinion, in the material they process, while the goal is still the same … Art was not a separate field of interest for me, addition to, or rest from, sociological prose. They were rather two ways of practicing the same profession, differing in the choice of raw material, but not products.[6]

But there's little in the way of sustained reflection on painting, drawing, sculpture. It would perhaps have been something to talk about in the email exchanges that might have happened. I was still in Leeds during most of the photography years, and had been teaching (and writing about) the sociology of art as Zygmunt's colleague since my first year there. I also collaborated with T.J. Clark, Professor of Art History at Leeds in the late 1970s, in setting up a short-lived joint degree in sociology and art history, of course with Zygmunt's blessing. But I don't think we ever talked about the visual image, in general or in terms of a sociology and social history of art. As Jack Palmer points out (pp. 40–52 above), Zygmunt didn't mix his sociology and his photography. When Tim Clark left in 1979 he was replaced in the art department by John Tagg, a foremost scholar of photography criticism, but again I have no recollection of Zygmunt taking an interest in his work, or in that of other contemporary writers on the subject: Victor Burgin, Simon Watney, Allan Sekula, for example. Also, the disciplines of visual sociology and visual anthropology, each with its own prehistories, were coming into prominence in the 1980s, and although in retrospect one can perhaps read some of Zygmunt's street scenes as doing the kind of work they focus on, it is very unlikely that he would have aligned himself with these (or, of course, any) groups.[7]

This reference to John Tagg and other experts raises the interesting question of Zygmunt's relationship to scholarly fields and methods. The question is a general one, but it is also a personal one for me. I have written about Zygmunt (and Janina) in other contexts, but never about the strangeness of my absence/ presence in Zygmunt's intellectual universe. Presence because he was my great supporter and defender for years – a complimentary external examiner for my PhD in 1972, appointing me to Leeds the next year, working to get me promoted twice during my time in Leeds, and throughout a great friend and frequent generous host. As he did with other friends and colleagues, he also took many photos of me, and, judging by my changing hairstyles, at a number of different sittings.

He made the effort to come to Manchester to my retirement conference in June 2010 (this despite his quite severe deafness – I doubt he heard much of the proceedings), and he was kind enough to contribute to a book published in my honour in 2015.[8] And yet I have no idea what he thought about my work, or indeed whether he ever read it (apart, obviously, from the PhD thesis). There's probably a volume to be written about Zygmunt's scholarly methods, and for all I know there may already be a PhD thesis on the topic. He was wildly eclectic, engaging with ideas across authors, disciplines, languages, as well as extremely (often annoyingly) frugal with footnotes, references and bibliographies. He really was the *bricoleur* of reading and writing. You can't – I don't – take it at all personally that you are somehow nowhere visible in his voracious reading, and very unlikely to be cited. Still – two particular absences for me are his 1978 book on hermeneutics, published three years after mine (which had been the 1972 PhD he examined)[9] and his discussion of the *flâneur* in 1995, with no mention of the *flâneuse*.[10] I am trying to write this as a way of commenting on his truly idiosyncratic (though – it goes without saying – brilliant and creative) approach to the advance of knowledge. Indeed, he also did not cite Janina's important essay on Gypsies when he wrote on the subject.[11] (And, for the record, I don't think this is a gender issue.)

Later our interests coincided again. Zygmunt's book on living in an age of uncertainty appeared in 2007, when my own book on the aesthetics of uncertainty was in press.[12] And here was a topic we could have explored in the dialogue we might have had. Because although we were both absolutely committed to the importance of uncertainty, and the necessary task in the contemporary world of learning how to navigate its sometimes dizzying effects, perhaps we saw it rather differently. For Zygmunt, the 'liquid' nature of our times (a concept which I was

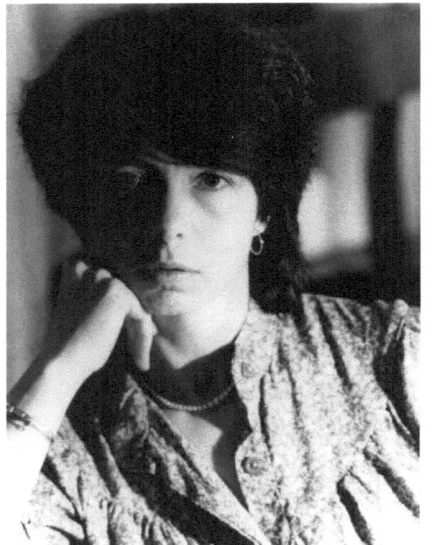
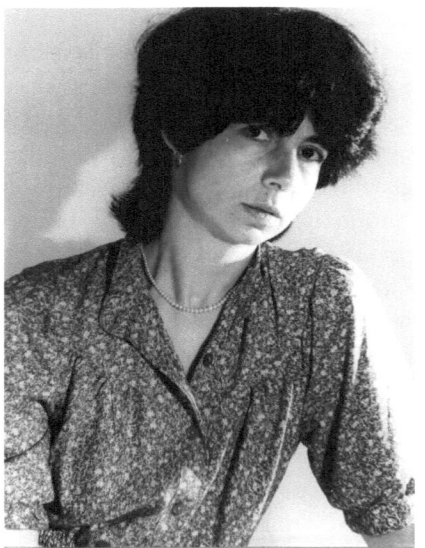

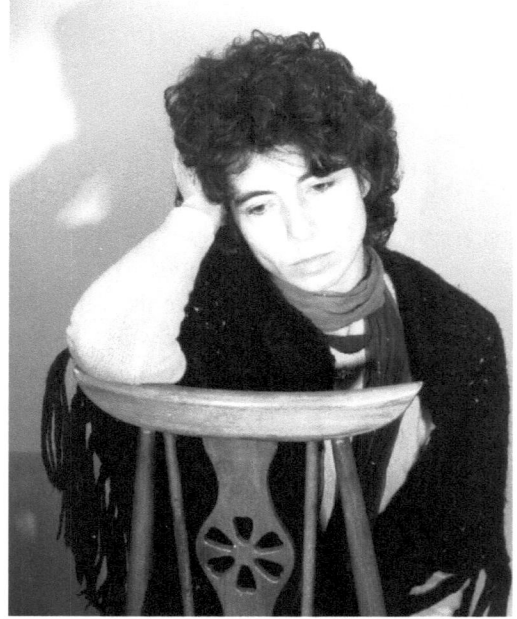

never entirely persuaded by) means that the old 'certainties' have evaporated – whether structures, beliefs, institutions, habits. I don't think he was nostalgic for that past, but he often makes it clear, across his many 'liquid' books, that important things are lost, and that the freedoms of liquidity are accompanied by a decline in social, cultural, moral values. The task, then, is to navigate the uncertain world, employing flexibility and pragmatic skills in a context in which encounters are no longer structured and prescribed. As he puts it, the current moment requires of us 'the necessity to act, to plan actions, to calculate the expected gains and losses of the actions and to evaluate their outcomes under conditions of endemic uncertainty'.[13]

For me, the embrace of uncertainty is not about the fear or paralysis consequent on the loss of old 'solidities'. Instead, it is the enthusiastic rejection of *any* certainties, and in particular those (political, personal, ethical) that refuse

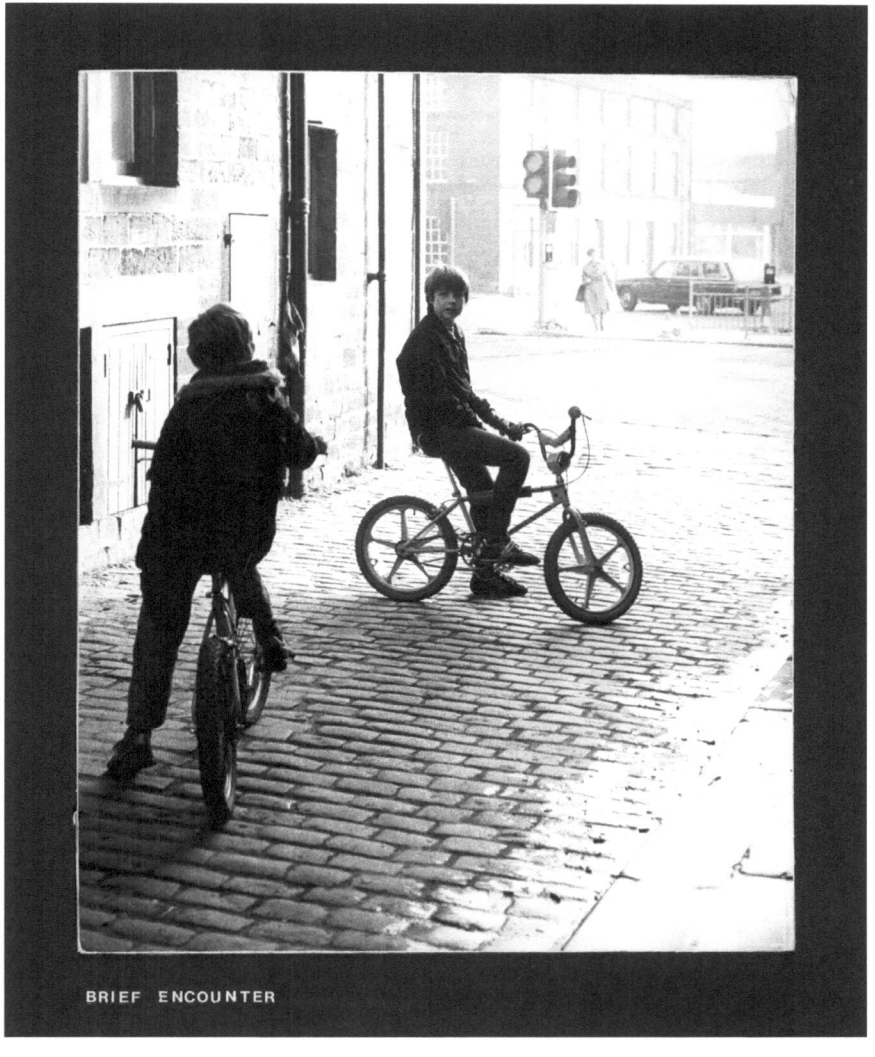

BRIEF ENCOUNTER

to question their origins. I suggested that the decline of certainty, a decline whose origins and causes Zygmunt has explored, is a moral and political good, insisting as it does on the refusal of unquestioned 'truths' and on the value of reflection, analysis and dialogue. But perhaps the difference between us is not so great. In any case, I know we would share a concern at the appearance of new 'certainties' in the contemporary world – ideological, political, religious systems of belief closed to argument or challenge.

In his acceptance speech on receiving the Prince of Asturias prize in October 2010, Zygmunt spoke forcefully about the task of the humanities:

> We, humans, would prefer to inhabit an orderly, clean and transparent world in which good and evil, beauty and ugliness, truth and lie are neatly separated from each other and never mix, so that we can be sure how things are, where to go and how to proceed; we dream of a world in which judgements and decisions can be made without the arduous labour of understanding. It is of this dream of ours that *ideologies* are born – those dense curtains that stop looking short of seeing.[14]

He borrows Milan Kundera's notion of 'tearing the curtain', an act that presents the world 'in all its naked, uncomfortable yet liberating, reality: reality of the *multitude of meanings* and irreparable *shortage of absolute truths*.[15] Honouring the heritage of his Spanish hosts, he follows Kundera in praising Cervantes, who 'sent Don Quixote to tear up the curtains patched together of myths, masks, stereotypes, prejudgments and pre-interpretations, curtains that cover up tightly the world we inhabit and which we struggle to understand – but are bound to struggle in vain as long as the curtain is not raised or torn up'.[16] But when it is, he says, we can see a world 'in which the sole certainty is the *certainty of uncertainty*', where 'we are bound to attempt, ever again and each time inconclusively, to understand ourselves and each other, to communicate, and so live *with* each other and *for* each other'.[17]

There are two self-portraits by Zygmunt, one with Janina, one of him alone, sitting on the stairs in Lawnswood Gardens. On the wall behind is an image of Don Quixote – a small metal sculpture in a metal frame. It's one of several Don Quixotes in the house. There was a black and white print, and a small wooden sculpture too. The homage to Cervantes in the Asturias speech was not just the politeness of the laureate, but came from a long fascination with the author and the fictional character, expressing admiration for the character who sets out, tries, fails and carries on.

There is another angle on the Cervantes connection. More than once, Zygmunt wrote about Jorge Luis Borges's story of Pierre Menard, who set himself the task of rewriting passages of *Don Quixote*.[18] Here his interest, like Borges's, is not in the character or the story but in meaning, interpretation,

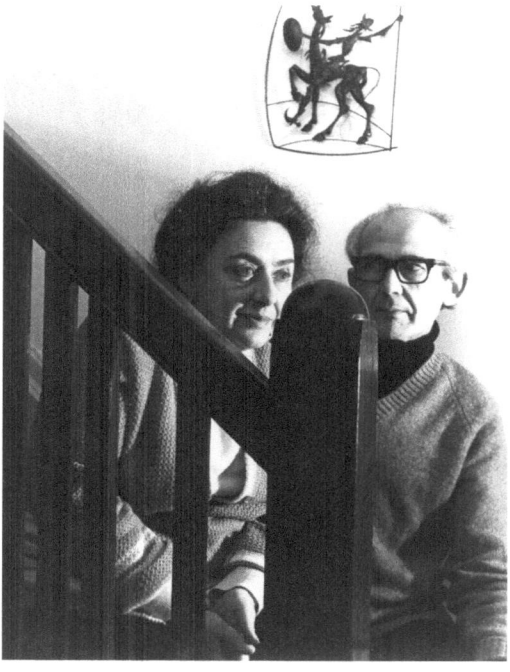

context and the intriguing recognition that the same words will mean different things at different times. In a wonderful essay on the theme of repetition
in Bauman's work, written as a strong defence against accusations of self-
plagiarism, Keith Tester reminds the reader that as early as 1978 Bauman
was making the case for the 'fluidity of meaning', the hermeneutic principle
of situated and unstable knowledge. In *Hermeneutics and Social Science* he turns
to Borges/Menard/Cervantes to demonstrate this. (According to Tester, this
is the first time Bauman explicitly draws on literature as more than a passing
reference.) Tester himself then employs Borges/Menard/Bauman in response
to those who have objected to Bauman's recycling of his own work – to
insist that repetition is not (necessarily) restating the same argument.[19] It's not
entirely convincing – I do think there are examples of cut-and-paste of a more
lazy kind in some of Bauman's work – but the principle of unfixed meaning
which he himself insists on can certainly rescue him from some accusations of
self-plagiarism. Keith Tester gives one example, of a reuse of text in *Postmodern
Ethics* and *Modernity and the Holocaust*, arguing that the new context confers new
meaning to the words.[20] His case for the defence: 'The meaning of a text varies
by its placement in the context of the work. *The texts and the work are not the same
even where the texts constituting the work might be identical.*'[21] Indirectly, and belatedly,
Don Quixote has come to Zygmunt's rescue.

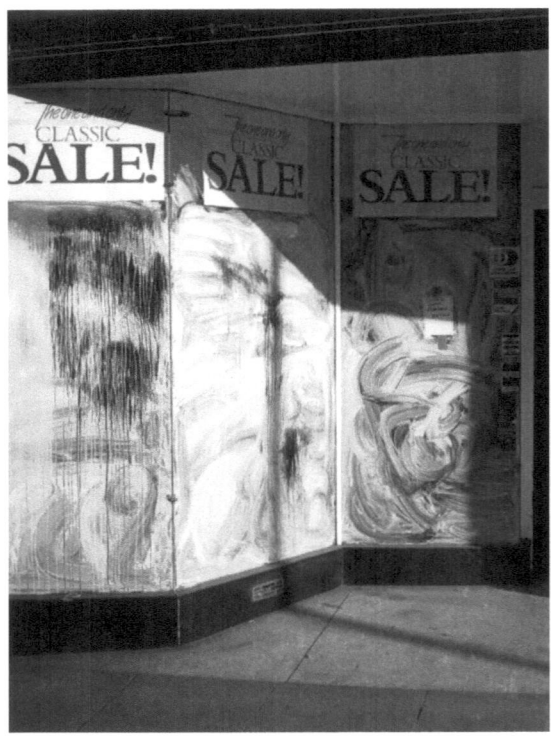

At about the same time as Zygmunt was giving up photography and, after *Modernity and the Holocaust*, re-engaging with sociology, I was moving from sociology to art history, at least in my institutional affiliation. For ten years, from 1991, I was director of a PhD programme in Visual and Cultural Studies, and found myself in an art history department, as a Professor of Art History.[22] My work and interests hadn't changed, but they would not have fitted so well in a sociology department in the USA. At the same time, humanities departments were taking on more social-historical and sociological (and political) approaches. In co-ordinating this interdisciplinary programme, I had a mission to incorporate a sociological approach, which to some extent was achieved by involving colleagues across campus in anthropology, ethnomusicology and critical film studies.[23] Inevitably, given my new context, I did turn to work more on visual art and artists (Gwen John, R.B. Kitaj, early twentieth-century American art, English Jewish artists). Our graduate students studied visual art across the board: painting, sculpture, film and photography. (I own some wonderful photographic work by two of my colleagues from that time, Carl Chiarenza and Roger Mertin.) Later, and especially after returning to England in 2006, I developed an interest in photography myself, and in particular in the interplay between image and text. The last class I taught before retirement in 2010 was Literature, Writing and Visual Culture. Like many people, I was very taken with the work of the writer W.G. Sebald, and with the placement (and role) of black-and-white images in his novels.[24]

In the dialogue book I might have done with Zygmunt, I would probably have tried to raise the question of the placement of images, the intersection of image and text, the question of how an image changes the meaning of the words (and vice versa). It wasn't something he'd expressed interest in, but I am convinced he would have had thoughts on this. The only example I know of where his photos are intentionally placed with text is in the community study book on Osmondthorpe, which Peter Beilharz writes about (pp. 12–13 above), where he was asked to take the photos for the author.[25] The recent collection of essays by Zygmunt on culture and art, consisting of previously unpublished work, includes an essay on photography, in fact a composite of various pieces – notes and short essays – found among his papers.[26] The editors have included six of his photographs – three street scenes and three landscape images. I think there is no particular intention to facilitate dialogue between text and image; rather, the photos are there as illustrations of his decade of photographic practice. They quote him as reflecting much later (2009) that his photography had been an artistic anticipation of his subsequent academic work on postmodernity, which perhaps gives us licence to read the images as social commentary.[27] Tony Bryant and Griselda Pollock, in their short essay (pp. 26–7 above), suggest that we can.

I am inclined to end on a Sebaldian note here. Sebald famously (notoriously) inserted random photographs, picked up in flea markets, into his books, alongside photos of the real models for his character. So you never know quite how to read the image.[28] At the same time, the images – often quite mysterious in content, and often a little fuzzy in definition – transform the reading of the text in unexpected ways. In an interview in 1997, Sebald addresses the question of his use of images by saying that one of its functions is to arrest time.[29] They can also disrupt the textual meaning (and vice versa). Helen Hills puts it well: 'Images detonate and throw the reader off kilter; text disorients the reading of the image ... Sebald deploys photographs like guns. They disrupt and knock off course.'[30] When we researched the archive of Zygmunt's photographs, we came across quite a few whose subjects were anonymous, whose conditions of production were equally unknown. This one I found particularly compelling. Conductor of a children's orchestra? Surrounded by busts of composers? Nobody I asked, including the Bauman family, can tell me. It's quite tempting to use the photo in some future text of my own, subject to be decided, to see what work it might do in dialogue with words.

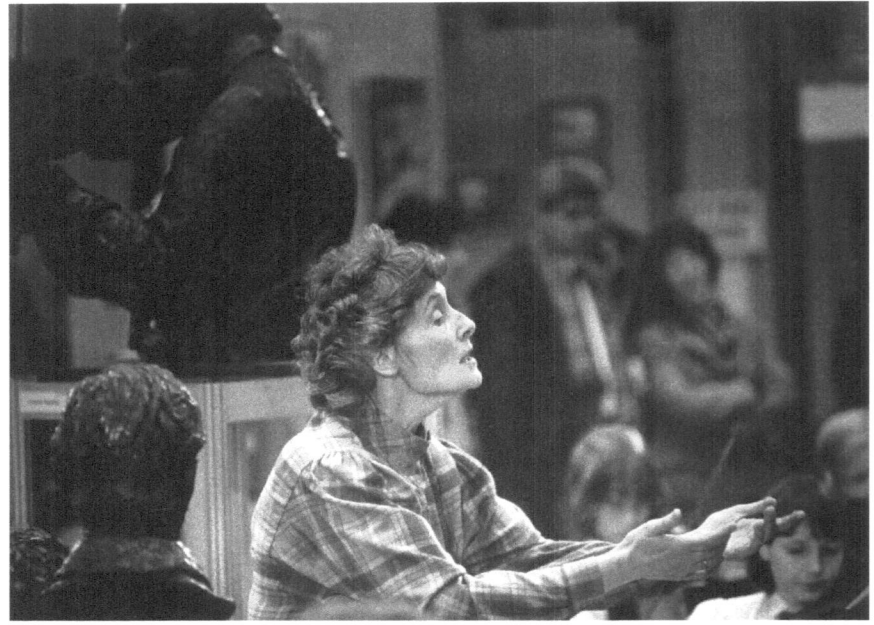

Notes

1 Janina Bauman, *A Dream of Belonging: My Years in Postwar Poland* (London: Virago, 1988), 157.

2 As I was writing this essay, I learned that along with five other sites the boundary markers had just been granted Grade II listed status by the Department for Digital, Culture, Media and Sport on the advice of Historic England, in celebration of the Queen's Platinum Jubilee. *Manchester Evening News*, 24 May 2022.

3 The outstanding exception is Izabela Wagner's magisterial book, *Bauman: A Biography* (Cambridge: Polity, 2020). The exception to the point about dialogue books is Bauman's *Living on Borrowed Time: Conversations with Citlali Rovirosa-Madrazo* (Cambridge: Polity, 2009). One volume co-edited by a woman is Jerzy Kociatkiewicz and Monika Kostera (eds), *Liquid Organization: Zygmunt Bauman and Organization Theory* (Abingdon: Routledge, 2014).

4 Zygmunt Bauman and Riccardo Mazzeo, *In Praise of Literature* (Cambridge: Polity, 2016). See also Bauman, 'A Few (Erratic) Thoughts on the Morganatic Liaison of Theory and Literature', in Dariusz Brzeziński, Mark Davis, Jack Palmer and Tom Campbell (eds), *Zygmunt Bauman. Culture and Art: Selected Writings, Volume I* (Cambridge: Polity, 2021).

5 'Einstein Meets Magritte: Postmodernity Is Born' and 'On Art, Death and Postmodernity – and What They Do to Each Other', in *Zygmunt Bauman: Culture and Art*. Though the likely Magritte homage in the title of his 2012 book *This is Not a Diary* (Cambridge: Polity) does rather miss the point of the original painting.

6 Brzeziński et al. (eds), *Culture and Art: Volume I* (Cambridge: Polity, 2021), pp. xii–xiii.

7 The Granada Centre for Visual Anthropology at the University of Manchester was established in 1987, but its first academic home was in 1958 at Harvard, with a longer history of ethnographic film before that. The journal *Visual Sociology* (later renamed *Visual Studies*) was founded in 1986, and the International Visual Sociology Association in 1981.

8 'A Few Scattered (My Own and Borrowed) Thoughts on the Fate of Intimacy, Friendship, and Love In Our Liquid Modern Age', in Cyril Reade and David Peters Corbett (eds), *Porous Boundaries: Art and Essays in Honour of Janet Wolff* (Manchester: Manchester University Press, 2015).

9 Zygmunt Bauman, *Hermeneutics and Social Science* (London: Hutchinson, 1978); Janet Wolff, *Hermeneutic Philosophy and the Sociology of Art* (London: Routledge, 1975).

10 Zygmunt Bauman, *Life in Fragments: Essays in Postmodern Morality* (Oxford: Blackwell, 1995), 131–5, 155. Janet Wolff, 'The Invisible Flâneuse: Women and the Literature of Modernity', *Theory, Culture & Society*, 2.3 (1985), 37–46.

11 *This Is Not a Diary*, 6–9, 25, 188. Janina Bauman, 'Demons of Other People's Fear: the Plight of the Gypsies', *Thesis Eleven*, 56 (1998), 51–62. Izabela Wagner has also pointed out that, despite his explicit statement that Janina's 1986 memoir, *Winter in the Morning*, inspired his book on the Holocaust, he never cites her in *Modernity and the Holocaust*, which she explains in terms of the very different writing projects the two books constitute. 'Janina and Zygmunt Bauman: A Case Study of Inspiring Collaboration', in Jack Palmer and Dariusz Brzeziński (eds), *Revisiting Modernity and the Holocaust: Heritage, Dilemmas, Extensions* (Abingdon: Routledge, 2022), 157.

12 Zygmunt Bauman, *Liquid Times: Living in an Age of Uncertainty* (Cambridge: Polity, 2007); Janet Wolff, *The Aesthetics of Uncertainty* (New York: Columbia University Press, 2008).

13 *Liquid Times*, 4.

14 *This Is Not a Diary*, 47. An incidental observation here. If Bauman had received the prize five years later, it would have been the Princess of Asturias prize. The prize is named for the heir to the throne, Prince Felipe when Bauman received it. After his accession to the throne in 2014, his young daughter, Leonie, became the heiress presumptive, and the prize was renamed in 2015. King Felipe still presides until she turns eighteen, in 2023.

15 *This Is Not a Diary*. Milan Kundera, *The Curtain* (London: Faber and Faber, 2007).

16 *This Is Not a Diary*, 46.

17 *This Is Not a Diary*, 47.

18 For example, in the essay 'Jorge Luis Borges, or Why Understanding Is Not What It Seems to Be' (1976), in *Culture and Art*, 92–6. And 'Liquid Power' (2008), in Tony Blackshaw (ed.), *The New Bauman Reader* (Manchester: Manchester University Press, 2016), 330.

19 Keith Tester, 'On Repetition in the Work of Zygmunt Bauman', *Thesis Eleven*, 149.1 (2018), 104–18.

20 Tester, 'On Repetition', 113.

21 Tester, 'On Repetition', 114. Italics in the original.

22 This was at the University of Rochester. The programme had been founded two years earlier, under the title of Comparative Arts, and I took over from the early directors, Norman Bryson and Mieke Bal. It was the first graduate programme in Visual and Cultural Studies, soon to be followed by others (for example, at the University of California, Irvine, and at SUNY Stony Brook).

23 The sociology department had been closed a few years before I arrived.

24 With my colleague, Jean-Marc Dreyfus, I organised a day conference on Sebald. This eventually led to an edited volume, *Traces, Memory and the Holocaust in the Writings of W.G. Sebald*, Supplementary Volume no. 2 of *Melilah: Manchester Journal of Jewish Studies* (Piscataway, NJ: Gorgias Press, 2012).

25 Alan Wolinski, *Osmondthorpe: The Area that Time Forgot. A Study of Community Work on an Inter-war Council Estate* (Hertford: Dr Barnardo's, 1984).

26 Bauman, 'Thinking Photographically' (1983–1985)', in Brzeziński et al. (eds), *Culture and Art*.

27 'Thinking Photographically' (1983–1985)', xxiii.

28 Or rather this was impossible before the publication of Carol Angier's recent substantial biography of Sebald, which exhaustively investigates the links between fictional characters and real people, and the authenticity of the photos. *Speak, Silence: In Search of W.G. Sebald* (London: Bloomsbury Circus, 2021).

29 'Ghost Hunter', interview with Eleanor Wachtel in Lynne Sharon Schwartz (ed.), *The Emergence of Memory. Conversations with W.G. Sebald* (New York: Seven Stories Press, 2007), 41.

30 Helen Hills, 'The Uses of Images: W.G. Sebald and T.J. Clark', in Dreyfus and Wolff (eds), *Traces, Memory and the Holocaust*, 63, 65. More recent work on Sebald and his use of photographs includes Clive Scott, Nick Warr and Nathan Hamilton (eds), *Shadows of Reality: A Catalogue of W.G. Sebald's Photographic Materials* (Norwich: UEA Publishing Project, 2022), and J.J. Long, *W.G. Sebald: Image, Archive, Modernity* (New York: Columbia University Press, 2008).

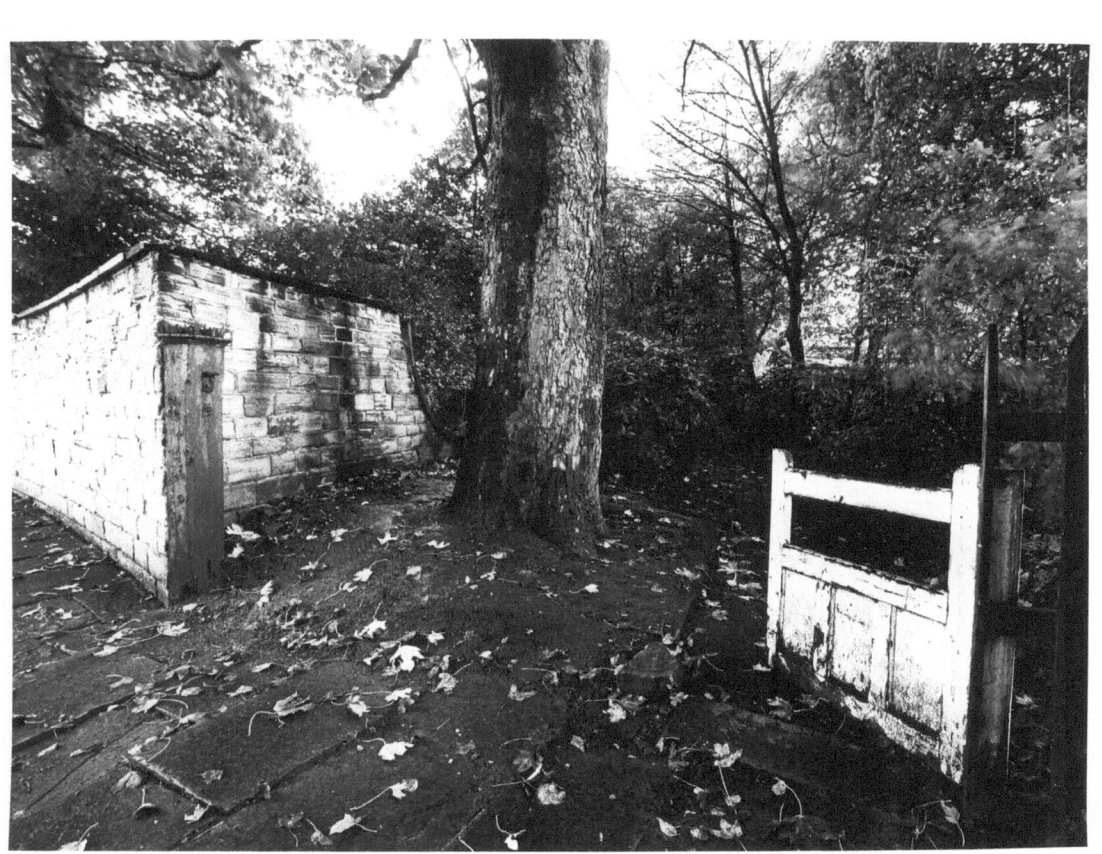

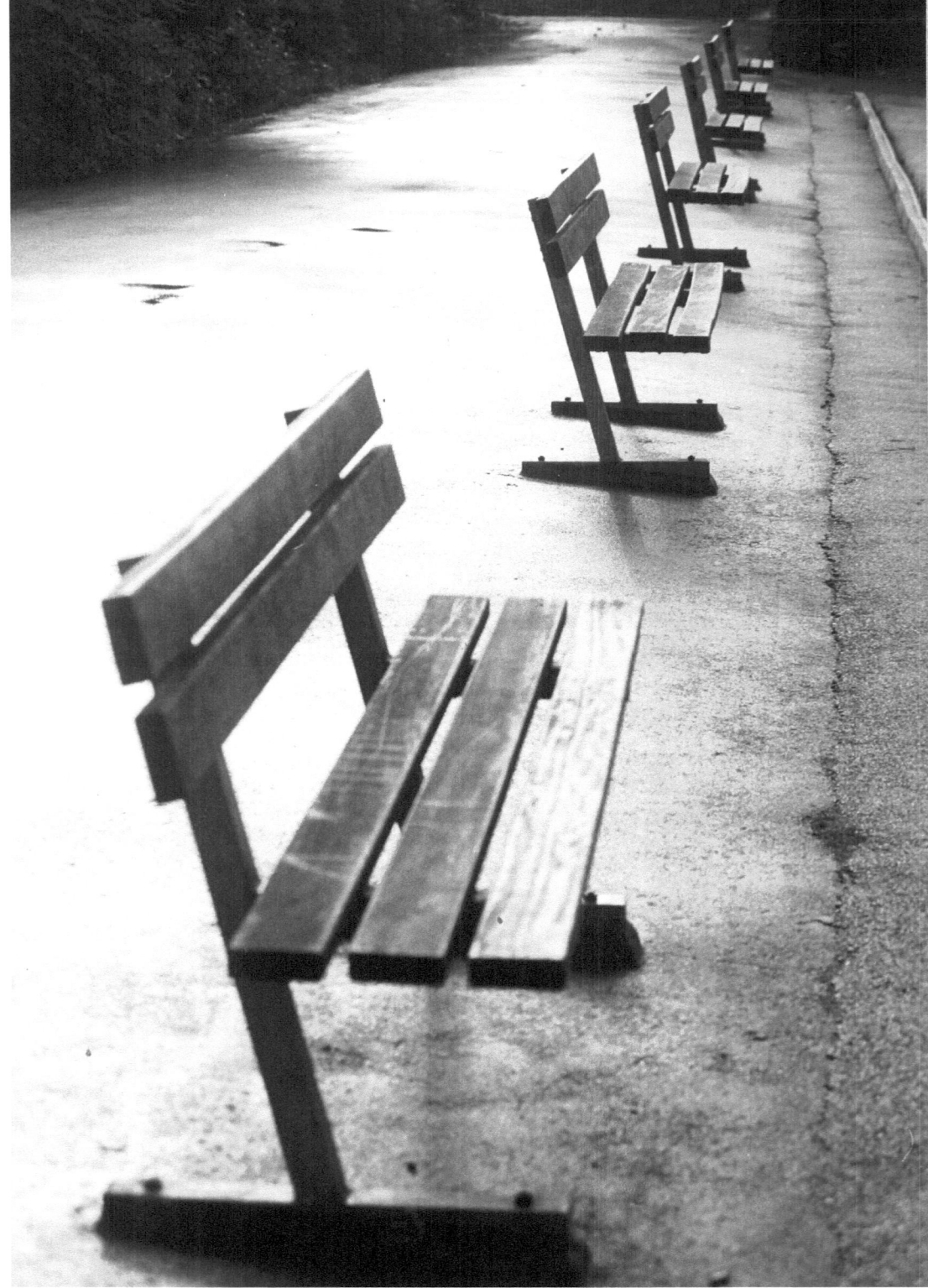

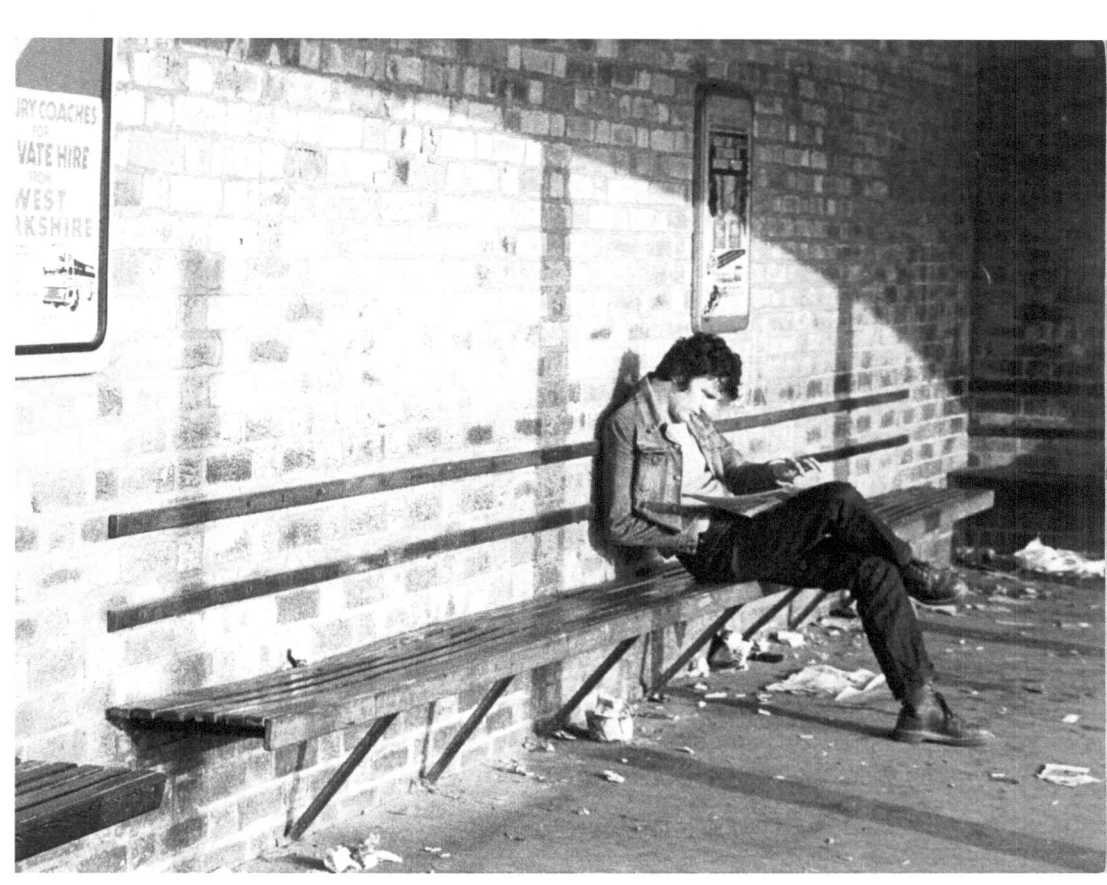

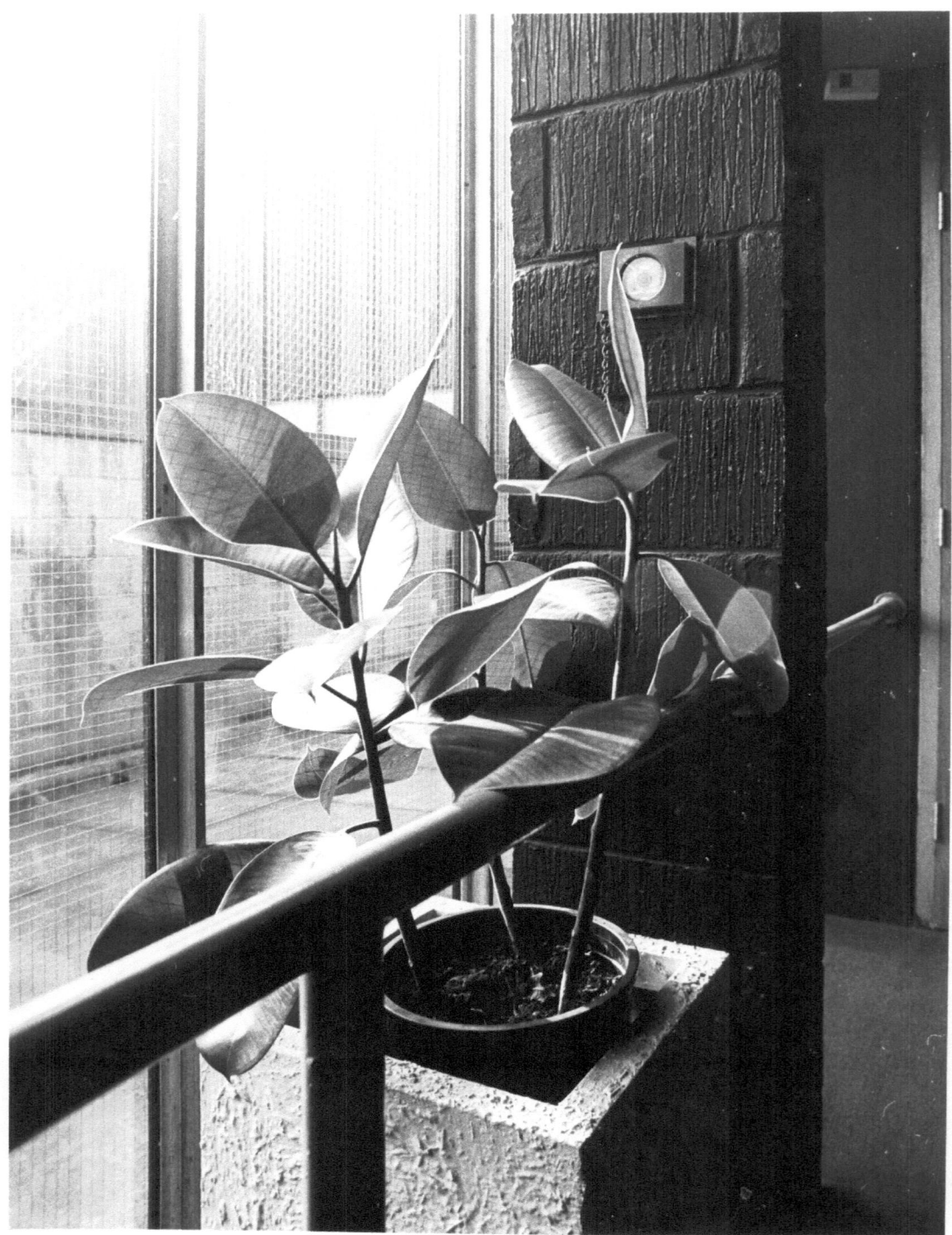

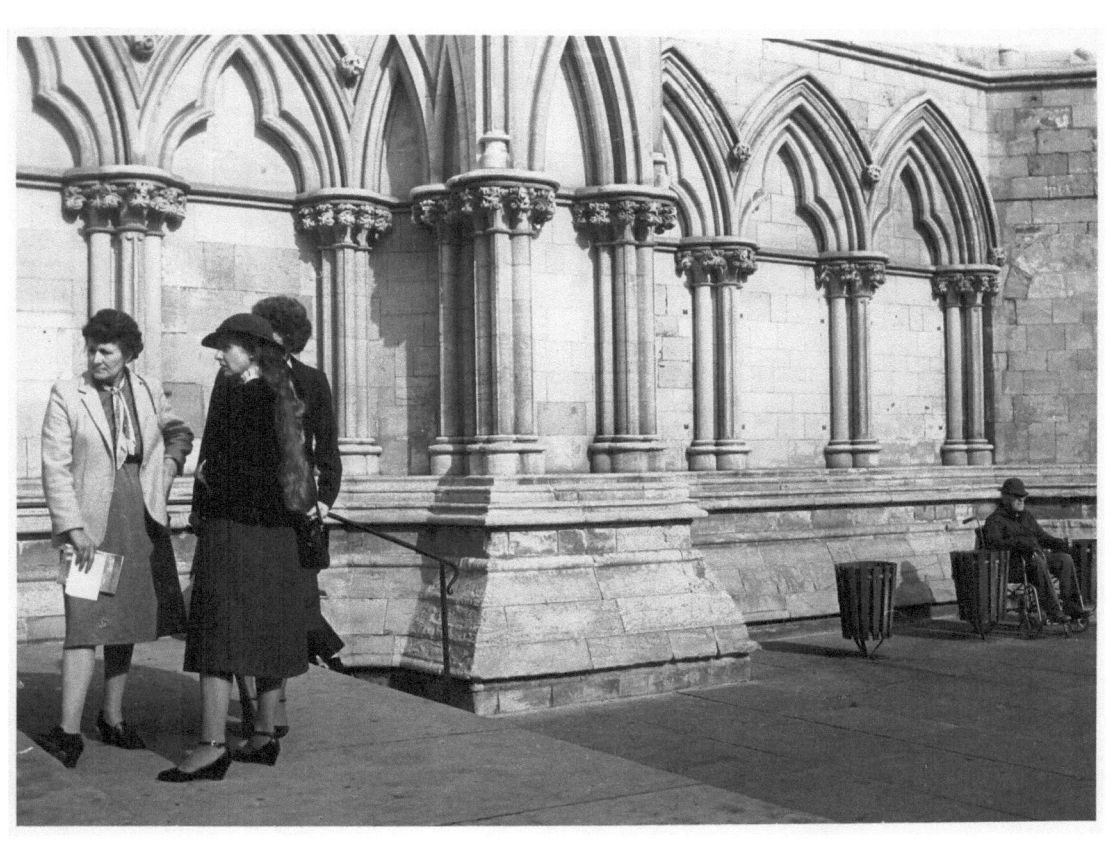

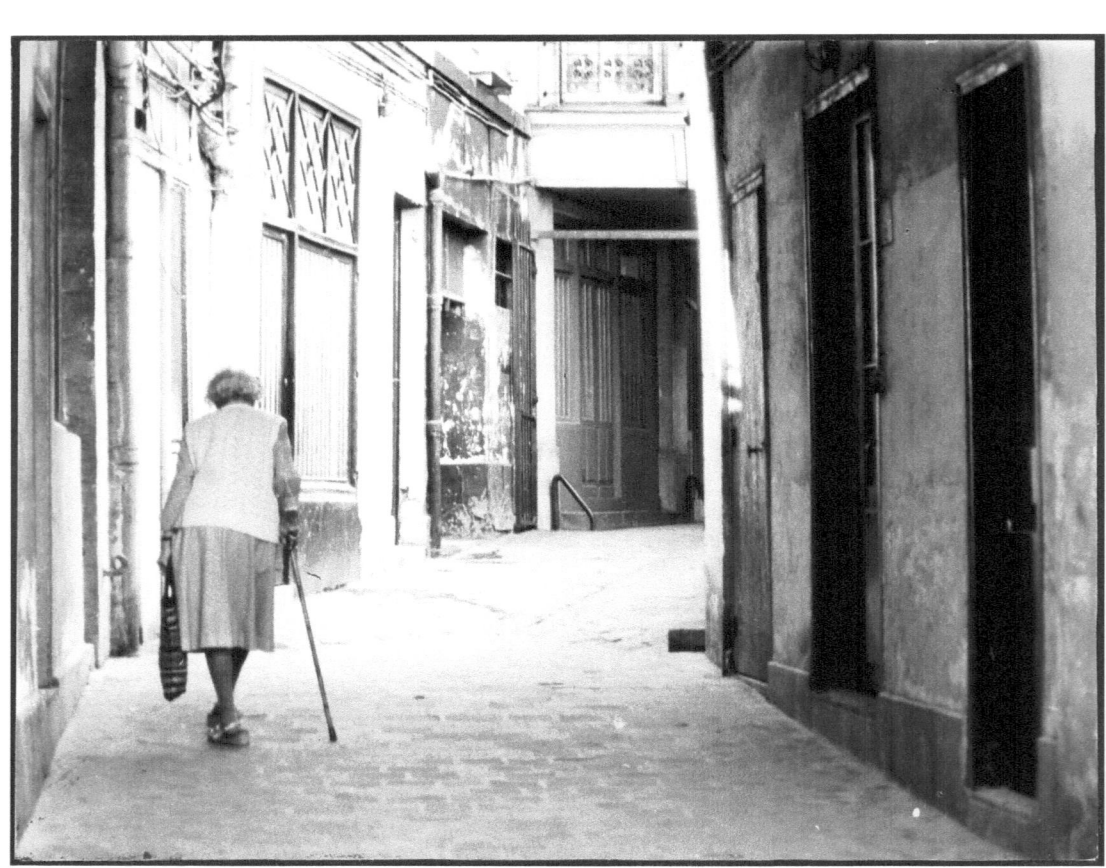

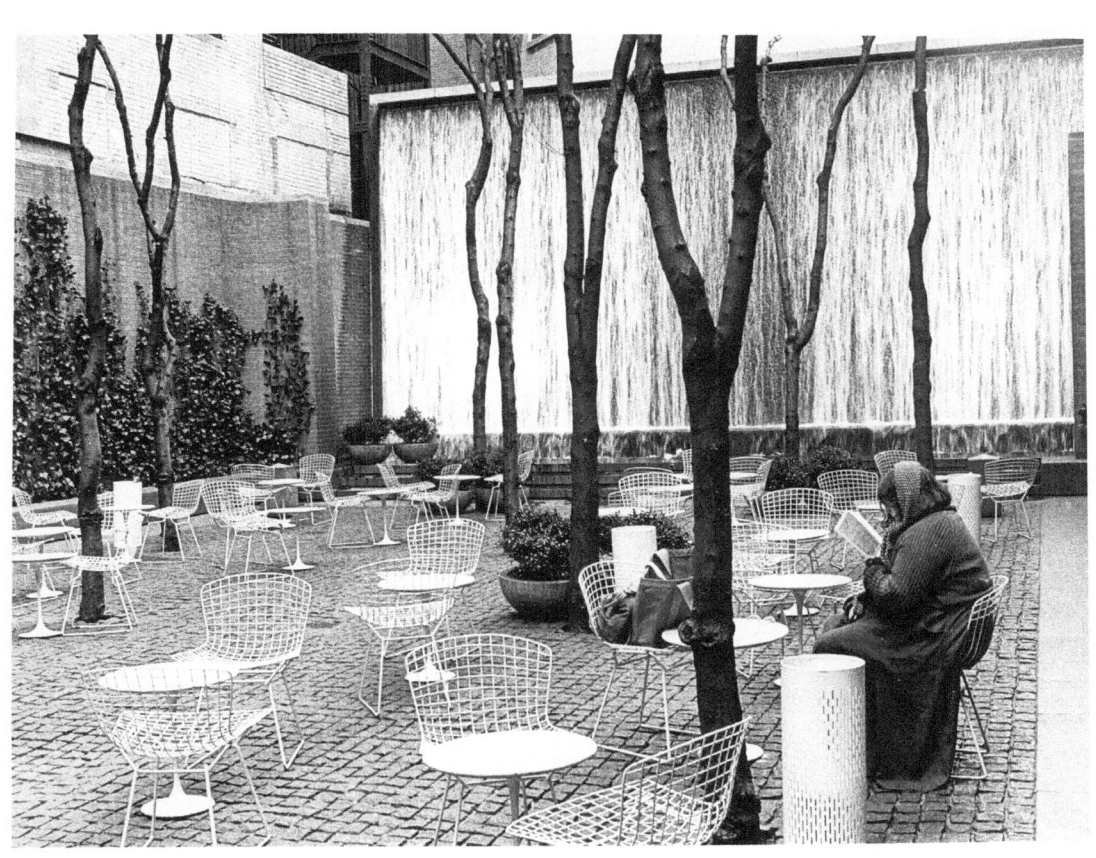

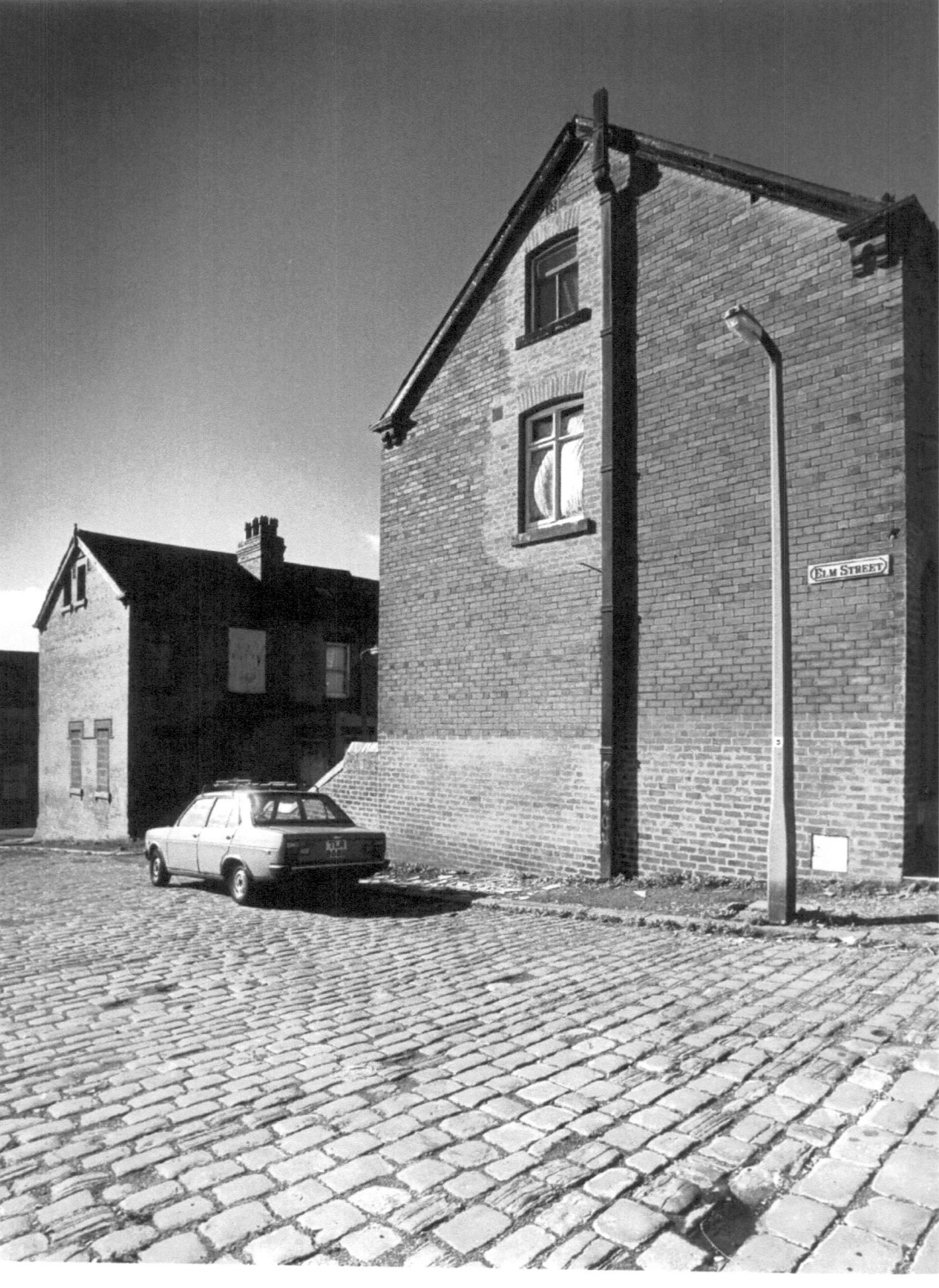

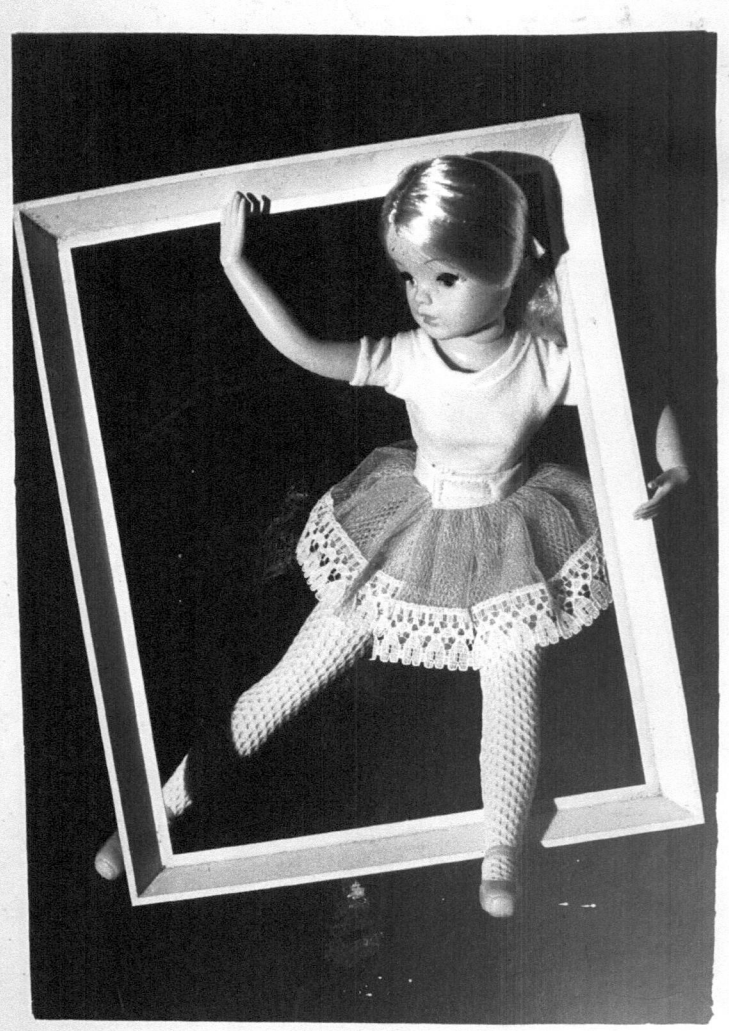

Mystery of freedom   [3]

The right leg behind the frame, the left in the front. For the hands, it is the other way round. She seems to be on her way out. Or perhaps, to the contrary, she is attempting to get in.

Look more closely. Is she really aiming somewhere? Who said the frame delineates a destination, a place to go to? Perhaps rather than framing an area, this rectangle is a frame of reference, a set of fine lines to perch on while deciding how to keep dynamic equilibrium and stay put?

Oh well, one additional glance and you get it: living on the verge is her fate. Whatever she does, she cannot possibly fit into the frame. Some may pity her, but she has learned to love this inside-out dance, this being neither fully here nor there. Once a source of her misery, this state of being nowhere-in-particular is now embraced as a source of power. 'On the other hand' became her motto: when one hand seems stretched toward one place, the other one is in a stand-by, always ready to turn into the opposite direction. While longing for order, she takes advantage of the inherent ambiguity of her unorderly situation. After all, with ambivalence comes control.

It is an unusually hot day in the middle of August in Warsaw, and I am spending it alone with my dad. These days, my mum is enjoying herself at a professional convention somewhere in the Mediterranean, and my little sisters are safely stored in a faraway summer camp. Dad and I are on our way to a nearby restaurant for lunch. As we are walking in the scorching sun, dad gives me a concerned look: 'Tell me, what person your age spends her whole days on her own?' I explain that all my friends are hiding with their grandparents, aunts or uncles in one little village or another. I have no family in the country. In fact, I hardly have *any* family. Father sighs in sympathy.

The plot takes an unexpected turn during lunch, when I spot a friend. Fresh from a visit to her grandma, she is happy to see me and I am overjoyed to see her. After lunch, we leave the restaurant together and walk over to her house. When I return home a few hours later, Father greets me with an ominous glance. 'Tell me', he says, 'what person your age spends so much time away from home?'

This is how Dad taught me about the hopelessness of the project of becoming a fully fledged member of any category. Never from that moment did I try to march into a single endeavour on both legs. On that summer day, Father launched a beta-test for what was to become one of his signature products a quarter of century later. With me as a subject, he tested his ideas about 'what living at peace with ambivalence may look like'.

Anna Sfard

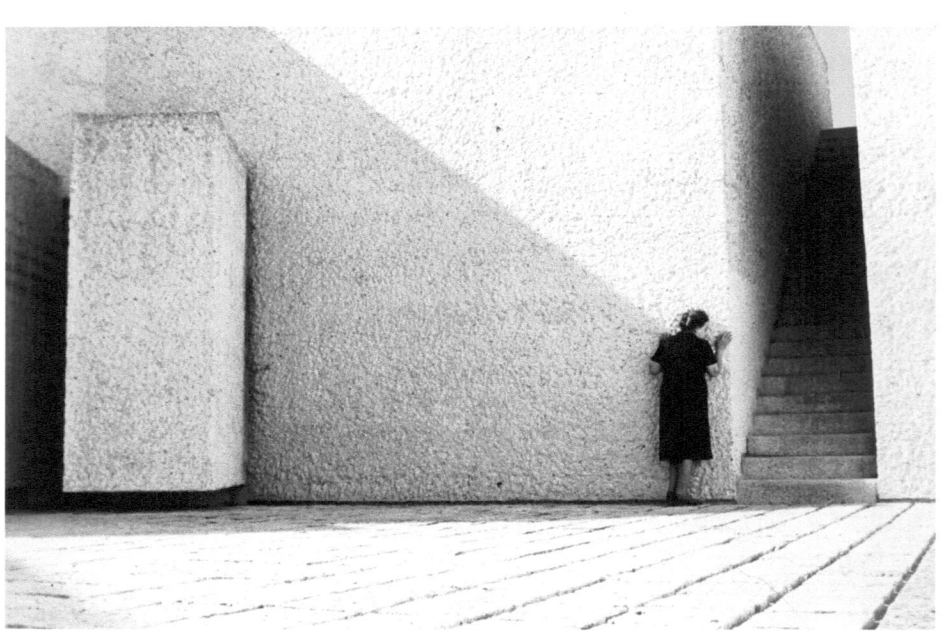

Straight, diagonal, parallel, perpendicular, triangular, rectangular, rhomboid; light, shadow, black, white.

Follow the shadow line on the wall which lines up perfectly with the tilted/angled shoulders of the woman. Another diagonal. A grip? Is it Janina, Zygmunt's wife?

Rectangular cobblestones, horizontal stairs, stairwell, buttress. Triangular and rhomboid shadow – the repetition of geometrical patterns and lines projects a restrained and orderly appearance in this photograph. The human figure draws the eye – what is she watching for? Is she afraid? Is she playing a game of hide and seek? Or, is she hiding, waiting in fear and trepidation? Is she a victim of the space, or is she holding up the structure?

It is not a calming image. Fear and anxiety underpin it.

Since first viewing, I have always been drawn to the orderliness and symmetry of this photo. Zygmunt Bauman and his subject would have waited for the exact shadowing to occur – to perfectly line up the woman's shoulders to extend the line of view. Her figure is both central and off centre.

He (or his camera) would also have been sitting or lying to gain the upwards angle, the line from below. It is theatrical, sparse, angular. There is an atmosphere of loneliness and a feeling of desolation – complete emptiness. There is no rubbish, detritus or plants, not even a weed in sight. Did Bauman clean the set/site first? Or was it vacant, cleaned by the hand or order of the authorities?

There is texture in the photo – the particulated cobblestones and the rough 'popcorn' concrete walls of the building add to its coarseness. And juxtaposed to this – the softness of the woman's rounded shape. Her black dress, its length slightly below the knee, the short sleeves showing just the bend of elbows and the curve of her upswept hair with contrasting hair fastener. The fingers curl just around the edge of the wall.

She is the human element in a sparse and angular setting, in the form of architecture that would come popularly to be known as brutalism. She provides the softness, but there is also something of sadness or fear here, or at least anticipation. The image suggests some suspension of time, and yet also a scene of suspense. It makes us wonder about Bauman at the movies. It evokes the clarity of image of Hitchcock, framed as perhaps in *North by North West*? Or are the associations more forbidding, taking us back to the set of *Nosferatu*?

The stairs represent a place to escape up and away or further danger, ever watchful of who might be coming down them. She is fixed, in a space in between, in suspension, the image held together by its framing, Zygmunt and Janina apart, yet together. And so they were.

Sian Supski

Janina Bauman in Film Polski: window to the free world

Izabela Wagner

Three weeks after my return from the mountains [honeymoon trip] I was already deep in a new job that I had found by chance. ... Barbara ... had a responsible job as personnel officer at the headquarters of the state-run *Film Polski*. Having heard I was looking for work she expounded at length on the prestige and fascination of working in this field. I did not need much persuading. The thing I most dreaded was working in a boring job, an office like the Fish Industry Head Office or the General Management of Milk Bars. So anything to do with films, no matter what kind of work, seemed thrilling to me.[1]

In *A Dream of Belonging*, Janina Bauman describes how she became an employee of a new cultural institution in the new state that was progressively recovering from the atrocities of the Second World War. This chapter covers almost twenty years of the history of Janina's work in Film Polski. It was a rich career trajectory performed inside a prestigious cultural institution, but also shows how the biography of Janina Bauman intertwined with Film Polski. The artistic output produced by this institution reflected both Janina's tragic past experiences and the postwar present. In consequence, she was not only a part of an artistic firm producing and distributing films but also a part of a social world that shaped Polish culture after the war. She was involved in 'national memory' transmission and the recovery of a society traumatised by the war. This was also an institution that indicated the future of a new socialist country. Janina Bauman played various roles in these crucial missions by performing multiple tasks. She had several reasons for experiencing a deep feeling of belonging to Film Polski. Janina Bauman worked in the state institution where in the 1950s the famous Polish Film School (1956–63) was born. Its legacy is considered the highest achievement of Polish cinematography ever and constitutes an essential part of world cinematic history.

Film Polski [Przedsiębiorstwo Państwowe Film Polski / National Institution Polish Film] was created by the Krajowa Rada Narodowa [State National Council] in November 1945.[2] At that time, Poland was torn by the home war. A new regime controlled by Soviet authorities needed to secure the support of the majority of society to win the referendum and legitimise the socialist government imposed by the Soviets.[3] Following Stalin's directive regarding the fundamental role of cinema in people's political 'education', the postwar Polish government created an institution that controlled all cinematographic activity in the liberated country.

Janina Bauman's various tasks

Janina Bauman worked for two decades in various offices and different departments of the national firm. She began in September 1948, aged twenty-two, as an office employee and quickly became a member of the team which worked on foreign movies; then she was the redactor in the 'script office' (from 1 February 1952) in Centrala Wytwórni Filmów (the Centre of the Movie Production).[4]

However, Janina's most significant contribution to the cinematographic production chain was her work on scripts. Political censorship determined all cultural production. Tomasz Lubelski explains that film scenarios were a significant issue since the beginning of Film Polski. Aleksander Ford and Jerzy Bossak were both first co-directors of the firm. They collected many scenarios (which they paid for), but many were rejected because directors were afraid that the new authorities would not accept such movies. Political leaders decided on production and distribution. Already in 1945 Jerzy Zarzycki proposed a script written by Czesław Miłosz and Jerzy Andrzejewski entitled *Warsaw Robinson* – a story based on memories of Władysław Szpilman, pianist and composer, whom they met in the ruins of Warsaw. The script was refused, and over fifty years later this movie was produced by Roman Polański. It was *The Pianist* (2002).

Work in the script office was highly political. The level of independence depended on place in the hierarchy. First, Janina was a part of the team in the script office (without a decisive role). Then she was promoted to a position at the intersection between the authors of scripts and the authorities. Her job was to help the former achieve their work, once accepted by the latter. She was in charge of correcting, advising, accepting and rejecting new scripts. With this responsibility, for several years, Janina Bauman was part of the censorship machine, an insider to the firm producing the movie; however, other institutions had the last word on the movie production and didn't belong to Film Polski. Despite being in that oppressive place, Janina is remembered by one of numerous authors who worked with her (such as the famous writer and scriptwriter Józef Hen) not as an administrative officer exercising her institutional power but as friendly, professional, helpful and supportive to scriptwriters.[5] This is not to say that Janina did not make harmful decisions. She described this specific job in detail, giving the example of the rejection of the script of the movie *Człowiek z marmuru* [*Man of Marble*], the masterpiece of Jerzy Wajda (finally produced in 1977). This critical auto-account of Janina Bauman's activity is a rare description of that job, specific to dictatorships.[6] Many more scripts were rejected than accepted in the history of Film Polski's activity (1945–68), and the rejections were not only the consequences of Bauman's decision.[7]

Three specific moments show the biographic connections between Bauman's life and the activity of Film Polski. Each moment is related to a film, and short synopses will serve as a basis for indicating the common points between Janina's work and her life experience.

Ulica Graniczna – *Border Street* – crossing the borders of silence

Border Street is a movie directed by Aleksander Ford, winner (Gold Medal) of the Venice Film Festival in 1948. The scenario, written by Ford, Starski and Fethke, was changed several times to make the story compatible with the expectations of the new regime. However, antisemitism could be shown only as a bourgeois attribute; Polish workers had to be depicted as good people, helping Jews in their struggle. There was no need to tell history as it happened (in the first months after the war, the authors collected several testimonies of survivors). After the final approval of the script, the movie was submitted, and again the authorities imposed changes.[8] The synopsis presented below describes today's version, accessible and available outside Poland.[9]

This is a story of the inhabitants of a Warsaw apartment house, situated on Border Street (symbolic name) and inhabited by families of different social backgrounds: a physician who receives his patients in the flat, in which he lives with his daughter Jadwiga (called Jadzia); an engineer with children (the older is a good friend of Jadzia); the owners of the bar situated on the first floor and their adult daughter and a young son; a cabdriver with his son Tadek and a tailor with his family – and grandson Dawid. The heroes are the children, teenage neighbours.[10] That big house is a metaphor for Polish society and reflects its stratifications: the doctor lives on the second floor in the beautiful apartment, and the engineer's family lives on the same floor. The bar owner's family is one level lower in a smaller flat, and two lower-class families (cabman and tailor) live on the ground floor and basement in poor conditions.

The movie starts with a scene from just before the war, when the children (ten to fifteen years old), despite social and religious differences, play together, while Ford doesn't hesitate to show the antisemitism that divides the children into two categories. This division was a fundamental social norm in interwar

Poland, affecting space, social relationships and children's games. With the German invasion, the cohabitation is broken, and some of the inhabitants must move into the Ghetto area. Departure is inevitable for the tailor's family (observant Jews). Still, the physician has a Polish name, and nothing indicated that he is a Jew. He has hidden his Jewish origin. The bar owner's family (Polish Catholics who declared themselves *Volksdeutsche* and were receiving German soldiers in their bar) discover the doctor's secret. Reporting his Jewish origin to the Nazi authorities, they take possession of the doctor's apartment, and the physician is obliged to move to the Ghetto. He sends his daughter Jadzia, who ignores her Jewish origins, to the family in the countryside. However, learning that her father is ill, the young girl decides to join him in Warsaw. When Jadzia is back on Border Street, she learns that she is a Jew. Her prewar friend (the cab driver's son) proposes to hide her, as Jewish people cannot live on the 'Aryan side'. Jadzia refuses this refuge and maintains her desire to join her father in the Ghetto. Her best friend before the war (the son of the engineer), learning that Jadzia has Jewish roots, breaks off their relationship. In this scene, Ford was also showing how deeply antisemitism impacted Polish society. The young girl will stay in the Ghetto and will become the best friend of Dawid – the tailor's grandson, a relationship that was impossible before the war. Dawid gets Jadwiga into the Ghetto with children smugglers and introduces the doctor's daughter to Ghetto life. Jadzia finally meets her father at the last moment of his life. Then the Ghetto Uprising begins. Dawid's uncle – a heroic worker – joins his Jewish fighting organisation and the young heroes try to escape death by leaving the Ghetto and joining their Polish neighbours to find help for Jewish fighters.

This is the first movie about the Ghetto Uprising of 1943. It is a realistic vision of Polish society, in which different attitudes are shown of non-Jewish Poles towards their Jewish neighbours. Theft or 'taking possession' of Jewish property, hate speeches and hunting those who escaped the Ghetto – Ford openly shows these horrible practices in his movie. The film was produced three years after the war, when antisemitic discrimination and crimes were still common in Polish territories, despite the absence of Germans.[11] Antisemitism was not only a past tragedy but also a postwar problem. By telling the traumatic story of Polish Jewry murdered by the Nazis with the partial collaboration or silent immobility of Polish society, Ford is not passing silently over the issue of the antisemitism so broadly spread among Polish society. In his movie, Poles are not courageous people helping Jews – or themselves the victims of German persecutions at the same level as Jews. In the late 1940s, work on memory could not deny obvious facts and still present social norms. People were still under the shock of the war. A male voice says one of the first sentences introducing the plot: 'Who didn't remember what happened?'

Certainly witnesses remembered, but few spoke about it. Janina never shared her story before writing her first book, *Winter in the Morning* (1986). As Zygmunt Bauman writes in the introduction to *Modernity and the Holocaust*, he learned what happened to his wife during the Nazi Occupation only from her book published in the 1980s. When the film *Border Street* was finished the memory was fresh, the survivors were still suffering and society was deeply divided. The administration of Film Polski had trouble making the film available to the public in Poland. Even though the movie was presented in Italy at the festival, Polish audiences had no access to it. At that moment (final correction to this movie), Janina joined the firm.

The story of the latest consultations before authorisation for the distribution of *Border Street* is told by Janina Bauman in her Polish version of the book; its absence in the English version is probably related to the complexity of this story. I complete here what English readers missed. After four months in her job in Film Polski, in January 1949, Janina was sent to the best-known Polish writer, Maria Dąbrowska, with the invitation to view *Border Street* and approve it before Polish distribution. In her book, Janina described this event, starting from the fact that she forgot it until the 1980s, when, in Leeds, she read Dąbrowska's Diaries, recently published. There, Janina found mention of her visit to Dąbrowska's flat (the elderly writer described Janina as 'a young lady from Film Polski'). However, the point of telling this story is not a nice vignette of Janina's only meeting with her idol (Janina had dreamed about being a writer since her childhood) but the antisemitic thoughts that Dąbrowska included in her journal. This is how one of the leading Polish intellectuals described the ambiance at Film Polski:[12] 'The environment in which I watched this film [*Border Street*] was composed only of Jews: Ford (unpleasant physiognomy), Toeplitz, some Mrs Hofman with a young man (husband?), and who was the only one *not to look like a Jew*,[13] and ... Radkiewiczowa [Janina's boss], wife of the minister of security, a Jewish woman ... very unpleasant.'[14] Then, after a short critical reflection on the film, Dąbrowska concluded that finally she could not fully convey her response to the audience because of the people around her. She wrote: 'I just forgot my tongue, and something like a fear took me away among these Jews.'[15]

Ford's movie identified a responsibility on the part of some of the antisemitic Polish population for the Shoah. Dąbrowska could be thus identified, and her notes confirm how deeply antisemitic she was. It was not a 'latent antisemitism' or 'folk antisemitism' but aggressive antisemitism, which, even after the atrocities of the Holocaust, was widespread among Polish society. Janina commented on this story in the following way:

Among many people whom Dąbrowska expressly reluctantly described here and elsewhere in her diaries as Jews, I lived and worked for many years.

> But Radkiewiczowa was, in my opinion, above all, a strict supervisor, Ford – a director of movies famous already before the war ..., Jerzy Toeplitz – an outstanding film historian. I knew that they, and some other filmmakers and officials, were Jews. I was glad because, in my opinion, it proved that racial prejudices did disappear in the new system.[16]

Janina Bauman was happy to be a part of such an environment – prestigious artists and professionals who could work in the national film company. This situation was impossible in prewar Poland, where racial discrimination forbade Jews to occupy positions controlled by the state. The Jewish presence in such a fundamental institution certainly influenced the feeling of belonging to this work among people who were no longer discriminated against. Even before the war Janina (at the same age as Jadzia in the movie) was the victim of racial discrimination in a public middle school, as she reported in *Winter in the Morning*. However, there is a more powerful element of the proximity between Film Polski and Janina Bauman than the usual status of disadvantaged minority. The history told in the films parallels her own traumatic life experience.

Did the scriptwriters of *Border Street* know Janina's life story? No. Ludwik Starski, Aleksander Ford and Jan Fethke worked on the script before Janina was part of Film Polski. Nevertheless, her story corroborated those of numerous Holocaust survivors from Warsaw. The doctor's daughter, Janina, had much in common with Jadzia Białkówna from the *Border Street* story. Janina was also a daughter of a physician. The family apartment (belonging to Janina's grandfather, also a medical doctor) was taken by his chauffeur, who at the beginning of the war became a *Volksdeutscher*, and chased his prewar employer, Janina's grandfather, from his house. Janina also moved into Warsaw's Ghetto, and, during the Occupation, she had support from non-Jewish Poles, as Jadzia did in the movie. Finally, Janina was also betrayed by Polish non-Jews and needed to change her hideout several times. All these stories from *Border Street* were part of Janina's life. And not only in this movie.

Ludzie z pociągu – People from the Train – 1961 – Polish society during the Occupation

This movie is considered one of the 'Polish School of Cinema' art pieces. Directed by Kazimierz Kutz, the piece won the Silver Sail in the Locarno Festival in 1961, Janina devotes a good deal of space to a description of the Locarno Festival as the meeting of 'east' and 'west', in some ways incompatible worlds. At the same time, she surrounds the movie with silence: 'well made and played moral drama'.[17] What is behind this laconic information? Why did this movie win second place? Is there more in the Polish version of the book? Not a lot: the film shows people and their 'various attitudes in this specific situation of them stuck in travel'.[18]

According to the official description: 'A group of people finds themselves stuck in a remote train station in German-occupied Poland. A drunk station guard gets paranoid, sees partisans everywhere, and phones headquarters. When the Nazis arrive, they find a gun, then threaten to execute every fifth person unless someone claims it.'[19] The station guard was German, and he is drunk because Polish travellers involved in several illegal activities made him drink strong alcohol, hoping that he would not scrutinise their belongings once asleep. Just before the guard falls asleep in the forest nearby, forgetting his pistol in the middle of the railway station, he calls German soldiers asking for immediate help. Before the Nazis arrive, travellers are waiting for the next train, killing time as usual for such a situation: playing cards, sleeping, chatting. Some people are nervous. A group of people is smuggling alcohol. Another young man is supposedly in the underground army and has a gun. Some women, street vendors or peasants, also have illegal goods to sell. A teenage boy is smuggling a dog that he has saved. There is also a little girl travelling with a woman with bleach-blonde hair. She is the special child there. Her behaviour arouses the curiosity of a man, who recognises that the girl (with dark hair and constantly trying to hide) is travelling to escape – she is a Jew. The man blackmails the woman taking care of the little girl. The woman gives him her ring, and he asks for more – her wedding ring – which she gives him immediately. This symbolic scene is passed over without comment: everyone here knows the roles assigned by war and taken by those who are hunted and others who are predators.

The blackmailer immediately joins the poker player, who, without a word, understands the origin of the wedding ring placed on the table as a bet for the next game... All these interiors of 'occupied society' waiting for activity are broken by the arrival of soldiers. The Nazis demand that the guilty men confess. No one acknowledges the crime, and Germans start the counting – each fifth person will die immediately. Meantime the train driver is looking for the drunken train guard – the legal owner of the gun. People's reactions to the danger of death vary. When a little girl is condemned, the woman who travels with her substitutes herself, and soldiers accept the exchange – the woman is taken aside to be killed, and the young girl will survive. There is no substitution when the younger woman is indicated for death, and her boyfriend (supposed to be an underground soldier) does not protest at all. People are weak and petrified. No one is able to save all these condemned persons. Soldiers are prepared to execute the death order, when the boy with the dog claims that the gun is his. Condemned people are liberated, and the innocent boy is beaten almost to death. The railwayman arrives with a heavily drunken German rail guard who recognises his pistol at the last minute. The guard will not be punished.

Based on a script by Kazimierz Brandys and Ludwika Woźnicka, this movie is not at all a heroic picture of Polish society under German Occupation. *Szmalcownik* – the blackmailer, who in silence extorts all that the woman transporting the little Jewish girl possesses – is a free agent. Nobody obliges him to behave in this way. Except for two people (who are not seen as heroes according to social norms), no one shows courage. The first is the woman taking care of the little girl and risking her life (we understand that the girl is traveling under a so-called 'Aryan' identity) travelling with the child. She heroically gives her life to save the girl. The second hero is the boy with a dog, who declares that he is the gun owner to spare other people's lives. Most men who are supposed to act heroically show no courage. This is a very unusual movie, completely incompatible with the national legend (and/or Communist national legend). Polish society under the Occupation was not composed of heroes.

Janina watched this movie, recalling perhaps her own Occupation experiences. Older than the girl in the film, she experienced the constraint of being hidden in minimal space. Did all viewers understand all the small details indicating each person's situation? There is no explicit declaration in the film that someone is a Jew. The blackmailing and indeed the permanent fear of being denounced – these situations were so familiar to Janina. It was probably clear enough – the movie won the second prize at the Locarno Festival. It was a grim picture of Poland during the war: a dark inventory of people's conformism, egoism and cowardice.

Wszystko na sprzedaż – Everything for Sale

This film by Andrzej Wajda[20] was launched a couple of months after the Baumans were expelled from Poland in 1968. In this movie, we see a metaphor for the end of a given epoch – the 1960s, as we know it today, the highpoint of artistic creation in Polish cinema. The reasons for this unique flowering are multiple. Historians and critics suggest that the censorship and specific regulation imposing such strict rules in the cinematographic production inspired talented artists to use Aesopian language. The consequence of these multiple restrictions was the birth of a new aesthetic, new forms of cinema, and a new language – part of a new wave in the history of world cinema.

Wajda (the best-known movie director in Polish cinema) turned *Everything for Sale* into a homage to Zbigniew Cybulski. This charismatic actor, the Polish James Dean, died tragically in his forties. He was a star representing Polish youth of the war – this lost generation not at all heroic, but lost in the darkness of history. The movie has several allusions to the war – the most obvious is the collection of paintings by Andrzej Wróblewski, a famous Polish artist who in socialist-realist style painted shocking war images of execution. The film is 'the movie within the movie' combining the information from real life and actions from the stage.

The plot is very simple – the cult actor (Cybulski) is researched by the women who lived with him and loved him. Both travel through Poland and meet his fans and collaborators and at the end of their travel they learn from the radio that the missing actor has died. We don't see what really happened (Cybulski died in an accident, when he tried to catch a departing train). This full-of-metaphors movie indicates the end of Cybulski's life and the decadence of the artistic milieu. The film launched in cinemas in 1969 and was very popular. The viewing public perceived this film as a vehicle of mourning, not only after the death of Cybulski but also because of the image of Poland itself as mourning, empty after the 1968 emigration, when, after the state pogrom, about twenty thousand Jews – the 'soul of society' – left Poland.[21] Its indeterminacy itself is a sign of the times. Turmoil came together with uncertainty, in life and in film alike. Meaning was elusive, in every sense, but you would still strive for it.

Janina and Zygmunt were among those who were obliged to leave. They certainly will have watched this movie in Israel or Leeds. It was the image of their lost home, a society that will never be the same, and times that will never return. It is a highly nostalgic movie which could be seen as the 'adieu' of Janina Bauman, closing her period with Polski Film.

Conclusion

For Janina, the moving image was central to her life. Zygmunt shared this enthusiasm, if not the vocation. He chose the still image, something so much in contrast to the movement forced upon them. They were both behind the camera, or the screen, in different ways. Zygmunt was eventually to shift from behind the camera to the front of the screen, as interviewee and talking head into his later years. Janina left film behind, in this professional sense, a serious price to pay for the relative calm of exile.

Life could be a play within a play, a movie within a movie, a vignette or a lament in a diary, a pastiche of words yours and mine. What all this suggests is that the visual remained a powerful and daily lens for both Janina and Zygmunt. They were serious actors in these different worlds, but also their keen observers. In the beginning, these were their deeds. Film was not only a reflection of life but a serious engagement with it.

Notes

1 Janina Bauman, *A Dream of Belonging: My Years in Postwar Poland* (London: Virago, 1988), p. 61.
2 *Journal of Laws*, Dz.U. z 1945 r. nr 55, poz. 308. Film Polski had various names. In 1952 the company was transformed into the Central Office of Cinematography,

and in 1957 into the General Directorate of Cinematography of the Ministry of Culture and Art.

3   See further Izabela Wagner, *Bauman: A Biography* (Cambridge: Polity, 2020), chapters 5–7.

4   IPN BU 1268/13431/1 Zygmunt Bauman, official document dated 15 August 1950, p. 6, in which he mentions his spouse's work. The Archive of the Institute of National Remembrance in Warsaw. https://ipn.gov.pl/en/arch/1555, Archives.html.

5   I interviewed Józef Hen for the biography of Zygmunt Bauman. Hen, born 1924, was one of the few authors still active in 2017; see Wagner, *Bauman: A Biography*, 163.

6   See Bauman, *A Dream of Belonging*, 114.

7   There was an exceptional period just after 1956 thaw when small productions were not censored. During that year excellent movies were made: https://wfdif. online/edukacja/wykłady/historia-kina-polskiego-wykład-5/#_=_, accessed 20 April 2022.

8   See Joanna Preizner in *Kamienie na macewie: Holokaust w polskim kinie* [*Stones on the matzewa: the Holocaust in Polish film*] (Kraków: Austeria, 2012), 13–43.

9   The entire film with English subtitles is accessible on: www.youtube.com/ watch?v=2ZD5E-pKKpY, accessed 17 May 2022.

10 We can find several similarities with the movie directed by Ettore Scola *Concurence deloyale* (2001); see trailer on www.allocine.fr/film/fichefilm_gen_cfilm=33450. html; accessed 15 April 2022.

11 One of the best-known was the Kielce Pogrom (1946), but antisemitic crimes occurred across Poland.

12 I am quoting after Janina Bauman's quote from Dąbrowska's Diary. In J. Bauman, *Nigdzie na Ziemi: Powroty. Opowiadania* (Łódź: Narodowe Centrum Kultury, 2011), 51.

13 My emphasis. This is a typical antisemitic expression and practice, in which people declared Jews were killed. Racial profiling was performed on a daily basis in Poland for a long time before Nazi occupation.

14 Journals were partially published since 1988. After the abolition of censorship, a total of 13 volumes of diaries were published in 2009 – https://culture.pl/pl/ dzielo/maria-dabrowska-dzienniki-1914–1965.

15 Bauman, *A Dream of Belonging*, 51.

16 Bauman, *Nigdzie na Ziemi*, 51–2.

17 Bauman, *A Dream of Belonging*, 150.

18 Bauman, *Nigdzie na Ziemi*, 124.

19 Synopsis from https://mubi.com/films/the-people-from-the-train.

20 The film is visible for educational purposes in the Polish language here: www.you tube.com/watch?v=LEp2k9MJqgU.

21 This emigration was important not so much from the point of view of numbers of people (between 15,000 and 22,000) as because of their cultural capital. See Wagner, *Bauman: A Biography*, chapters 10 and 11.

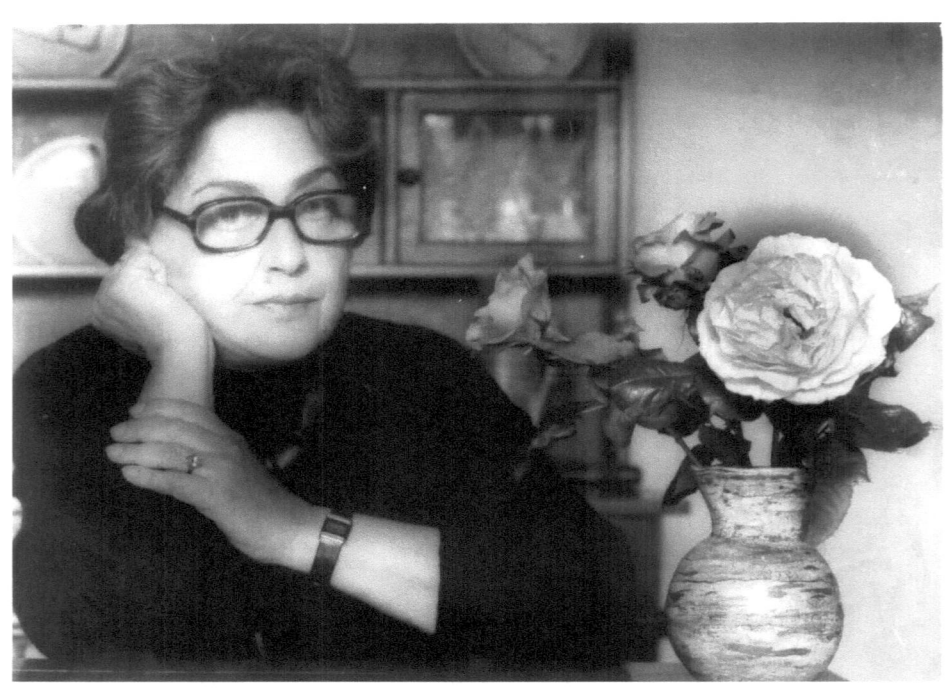

A photograph has the power to summon emotions previously unknown to us. An anchored moment in time that allows us to reflect. It was not until reflecting on this image that I understood what it represented to me; a bond between grandparents and granddaughter. They didn't intend it, but my grandparents' creative pastimes left long-lasting imprints on me.

Although I didn't often see my *Dziadzia* behind a lens, I was enchanted by his pantry-cum-darkroom. Already out of use in my lifetime, tubs of developer still sitting there, ready to spring back into action at any time. It was not until my own interest in photography began that I glimpsed his genuine love for it.

Once I'd started studying photography, each meeting with my *Dziadzia* turned up new kinds of gifts; once a book in which the protagonist was a photographer, next, a selection of photographs he had been experimenting upon. Until now, I didn't understand that these small acts were the building blocks of a bond, a shared interest that crossed the generational divide, a point of reference which we could use to understand each other. Although my photography career was short-lived, the bond it created endured.

And then my *Babcia*, captured here with one of her vases. A vase I recognise so well from all corners of their home; balancing on the end of bookshelves or holding a mass of pens and pipes. I spent so much of my time in their home staring at her creations, observing them, but never fully understanding that they were hers, and just how much a part of her they were. Each one skilfully handcrafted; a skill self-taught over time. Time that was most likely joyful and meditative, her escape from the world, her therapy. Long before I understood this about her pottery, I loved it for its aesthetic. The organic forms, neutral tones and textured surfaces, attributes I now know make up my own aesthetic taste, one I have based my livelihood on. And when I try to pin that back to something, I land here, with her pots. I am left with so many questions about my *Babcia*'s hobby. But my passion for it came too late, making this a one-sided bond that I'm unable to share with her. Perhaps, for this reason, it's an especially precious one.

I love to think of my grandparents, in their respective creative spaces, deep in their state of flow, doing something they love. This photograph is a reminder of this private side of them, one I didn't get to witness first-hand, but one that bonds me to them most of all.

Hana Bauman-Lyons

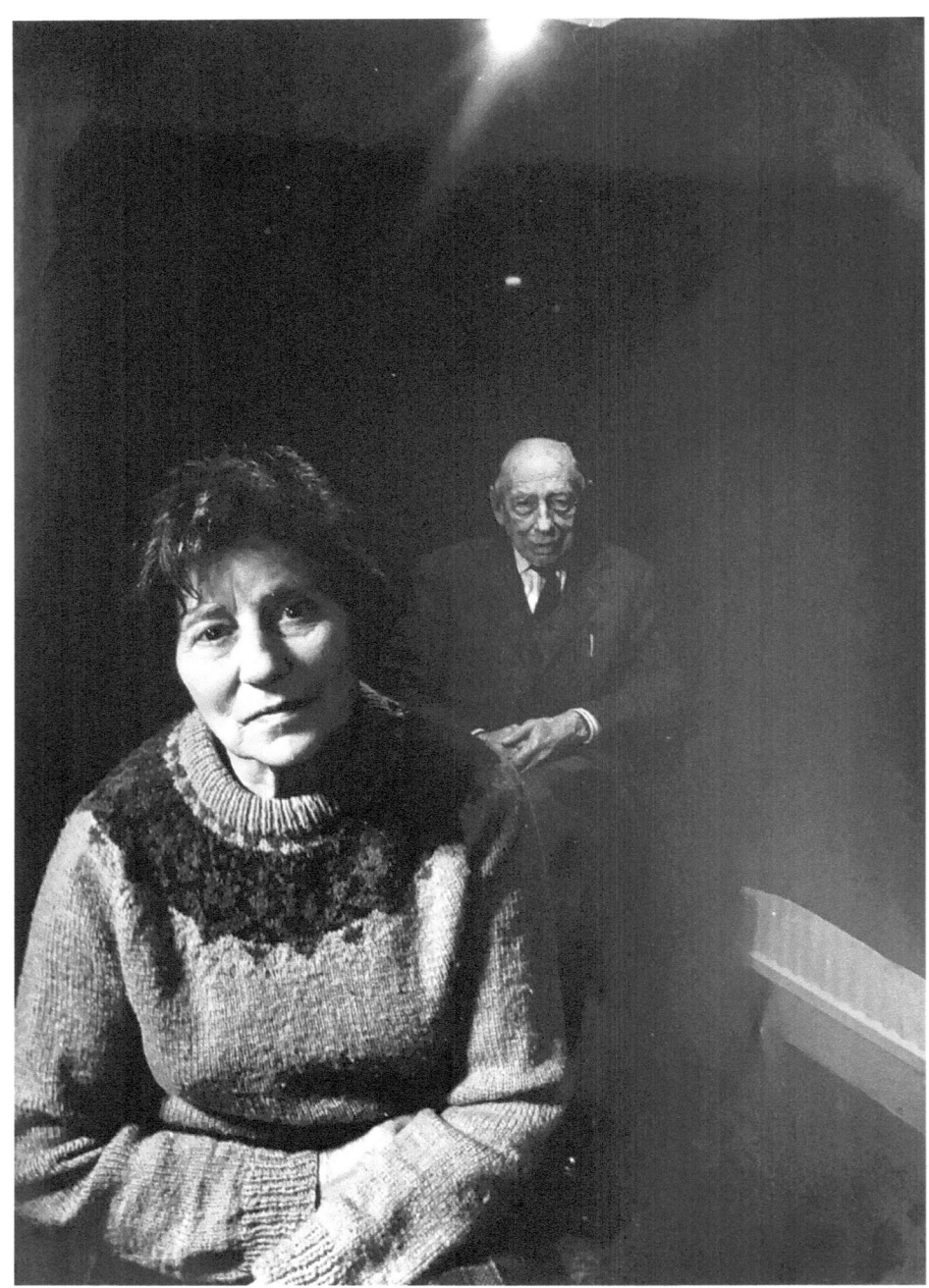

For an exile, habits of life, expression or activity in the new environment inevitably occur against the memory of these things in another environment.

Edward Said

Can one be a foreigner and be happy?

Julia Kristeva

From Zygmunt we have learned so much about how societies produce certain groups as 'other'. How ambivalence and uncertainty – human conditions which he and I both value highly – are projected on to marginalised groups, in the vain hope of gaining certainty and (we could even say) solidity. How the practice and rhetoric of 'allosemitism' (marking out Jews as 'other') result in the opposite but equally problematic cultures of antisemitism and philosemitism. How increasingly global processes produce 'wasted lives', and new anxieties about immigrants and refugees – the 'strangers at our door'. And thanks to Janina, too, we see how the Roma have been 'demons' of other people's fears in the West.

Zygmunt took photographs of Roma people, and looking at them we may find ourselves asking about the reverse point of view: what is it like to be excluded, exiled, marginalised, demonised? The existential aspects of exclusion are less his concern than the structures, histories, prejudices that have rendered such groups alien to us. Strange, in a way, for a sociologist who is reported (in Izabela Wagner's biography) to have been keen to introduce Alfred Schutz into the syllabus when he first came to England. But even then, the phenomenological approach of Schutz (author of a 1944 essay, 'The stranger') is more about the practical need for the newcomer to acquire the social and cultural knowledge of the host group than about the experience of being a foreigner. Elsewhere Zygmunt refers to the difference between *Erfahrung* (what happens to us – the outer world) and *Erlebnis* (the inner experience). It is the latter that I wonder about.

And I wonder, of course, about Zygmunt's own *Erlebnis* in exile – not so much his early wartime exile but his later double exile from Poland, in 1968 and then the self-imposed exile after hostile events in 2015. To Peter Haffner he spoke about his love for Polish cooking. It is Janina who gives an insight – briefly – into the experience of being away from home and in a strange country.

> The light, the scent, the sounds of early morning bring back memories of another life, another country. I left that country in the distant past abandoning all my young hopes and passions. Now I belong nowhere.

Hans and Bibi Schwarzmantel were refugees from Vienna, after the *Anschluss*. They lived for many years in Chepstow, Gwent, and moved to Leeds in 1983, to be near their son John, a colleague of Zygmunt's and mine at the university. Unlike Zygmunt and Janina, they were not barred from their homeland for twenty years, but visited Vienna frequently after the war. This lovely photo could be read as a portrait of sadness or loneliness. But my recollection is otherwise – a warm home, talk of politics, culture and literature, and a wonderful *Sachertorte*.

Janet Wolff

Bauman and Tester at the movies

Peter Beilharz

There is a photograph missing from this book. An empty room, featuring an empty chair. Keith Tester is an absent presence in these pages. The final doctoral student of Zygmunt Bauman at Leeds, he was to become his foremost interpreter. Keith is the missing participant from this project. Bauman died on 9 January 2017. Tester died on 14 January 2019. This dual demise was not caus-ally connected, but it was uncanny. Keith died way too young, short of sixty. He died too young to develop his own late style.

Tester said later that perhaps we never knew Bauman at all. Maybe; maybe we never knew Keith at all. Maybe we did, through contact, through talk and endless emails, and through his writing. He had a presence of his own, somehow gentle and yet firm at the same time. When he talked you would always learn something, as well as maybe share a laugh. For as both he and Bauman knew, much of the human enterprise was folly, a series of acts in the field of the absurd.

Keith knew about Bauman's photographs, but the especial enthusiasm Bauman shared with him was film, the moving image, and then literature. Keith recounted various early supervision sessions with Bauman covering the classical texts not of sociology but of literature; and endless talk about films. The work of the scholar in training was *Bildung*. Bauman would send him packages of films in the post, in order to be certain that his education in these foundations was sufficiently well informed. There would be homework. So Keith elicited those necessary desert-island favourites of Borges from Bauman, as I, at a distance, had heard on paper the resonances of Musil and Sebald.

Janet Wolff mentions (pp. 60–2 above) a proposed volume of dialogue with Bauman on culture, initiated by him. Keith and I had mooted a volume of conversation on film, photography and art with Bauman, but this was likely too late, as Bauman began to decline, and that fascinating idea of late style was to take on more ominous meanings. Keith in a sense began this trend of conversations, and its long tail, with that Polity volume *Conversations with Zygmunt Bauman*, shared by the two in 2001. This suited Bauman for a number of reasons, over the last two decades of his life. Likely he was getting tired of hearing his own voice, but also he increasingly wanted to share, just like a good guitarist will know when to stand back and vamp, in the hope that the others would step up and shine.

Perhaps, then, Bauman showed Keith different aspects of the older man's personality, as he did with others again and we hopefully each do with others. One result was that Keith began to work on a line between them, a small book on Bauman and Bergman, or more ambitiously on the mental screen he called *Bauman at the Movies*. It was a great title, for a book that he barely began but was keen to rehearse with others.

If photography – or film, or the visual – is in the foreground here, religion is in the background. Bauman at the movies was about God and us. This was not a conversation I was able to follow fully with Keith. While we shared a great deal, including Nick Cave and *Neighbours*, we did not share faith.

As Keith observes in the article that follows, on Bauman and Bergman, there are numerous continuities and connections between his two chosen auteurs. Bergman, mediated perhaps by Kierkegaard, takes us with Bauman into realms of vocation and communion, even to love understood as ethics. How should we live? Whose laws are we to follow? How do we choose our gods?

Given the opportunity to share, my Chinese students reading Bauman will most willingly talk and seek advice on how to be a good person. Here the reverse also comes into play: how not to be a bad person. Weber's sense of vocation was the standard German, *Beruf*. Tester rightly observes these connections to Bauman. As Bauman wrote elsewhere, there were also the illusions of a sociologist, who had the nerve to presume that their vocation, or position, entitled them to tell others how to live. *The Protestant Ethic*, Bauman said, was also about sociologists who believed too readily in the superiority of their own views or insights. This is why we are in need of the figure of the jester.

Movies might help you to think differently. For Bauman, these personal resources include the work of Bergman, Buñuel, Haneke and Carol Reed's *Odd Man Out*. Keith signed a contract for a book on these themes with Routledge on 7 February 2018. He had some ideas to develop: that Bergman offered Bauman an attitude to vocation, Buñuel a sense of shared attitude, or that Haneke was a partner in late style. In *Odd Man Out*, James Mason perhaps presented something more like an outlier, but Bauman had insisted on its importance for him when asked.

How might this book have shaped up? Keith also, in my experience, sometimes had troubles writing; but never with thinking. He had the Idea, a hint of something to come, of Another Bauman like the Photographic Bauman. We know that this was the world of Janina Bauman at Polish Film, and that it was a universe from which the two Baumans never departed. The epistemological point is both plain and profound. There is so much outside the text, so much to be learned alongside the canon, so much that we will never know or fully understand. Creatures of repetition that we are, we engage in the successive approximations of life over and over, sometimes looking sideways and up as well as back at those texts. We are always learning, even when we are learning that we are not learning. Yet there is also always something added in this process of repetition and mimesis. These were some of the things that Keith Tester left to us.

We thank Linda and Maddy Tester for helping to make this gesture possible.

Bauman and Bergman:
a short note* (2014)

Keith Tester

For many years before she was forced into exile with Zygmunt and their children in 1968, Janina Bauman worked in the Polish film industry. In some ways it must have been a dream job because, as Janina Bauman said in the second volume of her autobiographical writing, *A Dream of Belonging*, 'more than anything else, we were fond of films, and I was quite happy to spend all evening in the cinema after having seen three or four films during the day'.[1] Maybe Zygmunt was happier than Janina to sit in the cinema. She said he was 'an even greater film enthusiast than myself'.[2]

Evidence of Zygmunt Bauman's enthusiasm is scattered through his writing. The most sustained trace is in *Modernity and Ambivalence*, where Bauman shows a deep and perhaps slightly surprising knowledge of *The Omen* and *The Exorcist*.[3] A couple of years later *Life in Fragments* discusses Coline Serreau's movie *La Crise*,[4] and *Liquid Modernity* draws on *Elizabeth* to talk about the relationship between self-identity and mass consumer products.[5] *Liquid Love* uses Wajda's *Korczak* and Spielberg's *Schindler's List* to illustrate a point about the meaning of humanity.[6] The French director Robert Bresson is mentioned in one of the conversations with Citlali Rovirosa-Madrazo making up *Living on Borrowed Time*,[7] and along with Bresson the Dardennes brothers appear in the *44 Letters from the Liquid Modern World*.[8] *What Use Is Sociology?* shows a deep engagement with the films of Michael Haneke.[9] Meanwhile, *Thinking Sociologically* uses the end credits of a film as a rather neat way of illustrating the role of classification in the construction of ordered social life, and of furthermore making a point about how some people involved in the production process are unnamed, consigned to invisibility.[10] Given how Bauman has always sought inspiration from a wide range of cultural resources, without care about what academic boundaries might establish as legitimate or not,[11] it is scarcely surprising that films have been useful for the development of his sociological imagination.

When asked what his 'desert island' book would be, Bauman chose a short story by Borges, 'The Garden of Forking Paths'.[12] The shadow of the Borges story haunts Bauman's work. It explores the tension between the straight-line pursuits of instrumentality in which time is about 'what happens next', and the human potential to create 'diverse futures, diverse times which themselves proliferate and fork'.[13] The story is a meditation on how, despite the demands of this world, the future might be rescued from predetermination. This is precisely the charge of Bauman's definition of culture as 'a knife pressed against the future' cutting into erstwhile necessity naturalised as 'common sense'. For Bauman culture is like a knife refuting the apprehension of society as an independent object permitting of no alternatives to 'what must be done'.[14]

Yet only to ask about a desert-island *book* reflects a latent assumption about the primacy of reading pages over reading other kinds of texts in the development of a writer. The influence of films for the formation of Bauman's thought has been left unexplored. What might Bauman's desert-island movies be? In the course of preparing *Conversations with Zygmunt Bauman* many anecdotes emerged but one has continued to provoke, inviting further investigation. Bauman identified Ingmar Bergman's *Winter Light* as a film of particular importance to him.[15]

Bergman's *Winter Light* was released in 1962. It was made after 1961's *Through a Glass Darkly*, and was followed in 1963 by *The Silence*. (The film scripts were published in a single volume in 1969.) They are often seen as a trilogy about faith, thanks to a statement Bergman once made about the connections between them. However he subsequently moved away from this family resemblance. He said it, 'was a *Schnaps-Idee*, as the Bavarians say, meaning that it's an idea found at the bottom of a glass of alcohol'.[16] Yet Bergman never doubted one thing about the films. Or at least he never doubted one thing about the middle part of the erstwhile trilogy. He was quite clear and consistent in his praise of *Winter Light*. In 1966 he said the film was the only one he had managed to make how he wanted to make it. In 1971 the point was repeated: 'I think I have made just one picture that I really like, and that was *Winter Light* ... That is my only picture about which I feel that I have started here and ended there and that everything along the way has obeyed me.'[17] Although Bergman rarely watched his own films, he said that seeing *Winter Light* was 'satisfying' because 'nothing in it has eroded or broken down'.[18]

The narrative of the film can be outlined fairly straightforwardly. *Winter Light* tells of a day in the life of Tomas Ericsson, a sickly pastor who goes through the motions of holding communion for an ever-decreasing congregation. Since the death of his wife he has closed in on himself, and has become incapable of communication. Tomas's inability to understand the fears of one of his communicants leads to the parishioner's suicide, and he treats Märta, the woman who loves him and with whom he has fairly recently lived, cruelly. Tomas is a man who has put up barriers between himself and the world. More than just sickly, he is pretty much dead. Bergman said Tomas, 'is dying emotionally. He exists beyond love, actually beyond all human relations … His hell, because he truly lives in hell, is that he recognizes his situation.'[19] However, simply on account of her refusal to turn away from Tomas Märta manages to get through the barriers. Tomas asks her to accompany him as he travels to give another service; Märta drives the car. She is the only person in the congregation for this second service. Despite the temptation to cancel, Tomas goes ahead after encouragement from the verger, Algot. The film ends with an extraordinary shot, in which Tomas recites the first words of the service in front of an empty church, and it appears as if his face almost *vibrates* with a new-found life, albeit a life cautious, disturbing and maybe unwelcome. He has let love in and been cured of his sickness unto death (the allusion to Kierkegaard is quite deliberate).[20] With this ending, *Winter Light* implies a recapitulation of the announcement at the end of *Through a Glass Darkly* that 'God is love'.

It would be foolish to deny the theological weight of Bergman's film. If God is love, if Tomas Ericsson is resurrected by love, then it is a short step to the assertion that as a pastor Tomas is brought back to life through the grace of God. But Bergman is too subtle to be so simply didactic: 'If one has religious faith, one could say that God has spoken to him. If one does not believe in God, one might prefer to say that Märta Lundberg and Algot Frövik are two people who help raise a fellow human being who has fallen and is digging his own grave.'[21] Consequently, Bergman opens the space for an approach to *Winter Light* which would interpret it as a story about how the love extended to us by the other, how the love they give regardless of the costs to themselves, is essential to our own capacity to live. By this reading *Winter Light* is a film about love as redemption, love as ethics.

Bergman summed up the position in a way which is not too far from the temper, if not indeed the normative assumptions, of Bauman's work on love: 'What matters most of all in life is being able to make that contact with another human. Otherwise you are dead, like so many people today are dead.' He went on: 'But if you can take that first step toward communication, toward understanding, toward love, then no matter how difficult the future may be – and have no illusions, even with all the love in the world, living can be hellishly difficult – then you are saved. This is all that really matters, isn't it?'[22]

Bauman might not go so far as to identify redemption through love as *all* that matters, but he most certainly agrees that without it existence can scarcely be called life. For him love is the pre-eminent form of being for the other without self-interest. For Bauman love is of the essence of being human and of human being.[23] And yet – truth to tell – if this is the sole charge of *Winter Light* it is not too original. If the film is just making a point about love being the prerequisite of the humanity of the other and the self alike regardless of self-interest, it is saying something Bauman could easily have got from elsewhere. Furthermore, Bergman's film was released in 1962 when Bauman's sociological radar was not attuned to questions of love or ethics. (Bauman's sociological interests around 1962 are explored in Tester and Jacobsen's *Bauman before Postmodernity*.)[24] So either the charge of Bergman's film was extraordinarily long-burning or there must be something else about *Winter Light*, some other drama, speaking directly to Bauman's sociological imagination. The clue to the other drama, the drama which traces through to Bauman, is provided by an anecdote Bergman gave about the background to *Winter Light*.

One day, when the film was ready to shoot except for its lack of an ending, Ingmar Bergman invited his father, who was a Lutheran pastor, to accompany him on a Sunday tour of some country churches. They arrived at one church where there was a congregation of four people, the minister nowhere to be seen. Eventually, to the screech of car tyres outside, the minister rushed into the church. He turned to the congregation, told them he was ill and therefore would only give a short service, one without communion. Bergman's father was out-raged. He went to the vestry, had words with the minister and churchwarden and took the service – with communion – himself. Bergman summed up the meaning of this little story: 'Thus I was given the end of *Winter Light* and the codification of a rule I have always followed and was to follow from then on: *irrespective of everything, you will hold your communion*.'[25]

What Bergman took from his father and fed into the end of *Winter Light* was an emphasis on *vocation* as a calling to do what one is appointed to do. In theo-logical terms the appointment is made by God. The Lutheran tradition upheld by Bergman's father and indeed by Tomas Ericsson defines vocation through the prism of Paul's First Letter to the Corinthians, where it is written: 'But as God hath distributed to everyman, as the Lord hath called every one, so let him walk' (1 Corinthians 7: 17) and 'Let every man abide in the same calling wherein he was called' (1 Corinthians 7: 20). According to the lessons of Corinthians, Tomas Ericsson has been called to be a pastor by God, and therefore he is obliged to uphold this vocation. Indeed, to deny the calling is also to deny oneself, a denial which is, by a theological reading of *Winter Light*, the cause of Tomas Ericsson's illness. Put another way, the acceptance of the call to vocation is a kind of salvation.

Sociologists are familiar with the theological concepts of vocation and call-ing because Max Weber made them central to his analysis of the Protestant Ethic. According to Weber the idea of the calling, which gave emergent capital-ism an ethical legitimacy, has come to be stripped of any salvational aspect. As he famously put it, the world created by the workers of the calling has become a cage.[26] But towards the end of his life Weber hinted that maybe a vocation could still be pursued if it was identified as response to an inner calling rather than a supernatural one. When Weber identified politics and science as vocations he gave them both a salvific dimension. They can save the self from the chill winds of the worlds of power and disenchantment. Vocations put iron in the soul. For instance: 'Only he has the calling for politics who is sure that he shall not crumble when the world from his point of view is too stupid or too base for what he wants to offer. Only he who in the face of all this can say "In spite of all!" has the calling for politics.'[27] Meanwhile science as a vocation offers a chance to stand firm against the very world science has produced. As Weber famously said, science cannot answer questions of meaning, but to embrace the absence of meaning is, in a paradox worthy of Camus on suicide, itself a kind of meaning. Science as a vocation is a way of coming to terms with 'the fate of the times like a man'.[28]

A similar temperament runs through the nearest thing Bauman has ever made to a sustained argument for sociology as a vocation. In his Inaugural Lecture at the University of Leeds, Bauman identified sociology as a discipline dialectically – and difficultly – placed between art and science. From science it took the commitment to reason, and from art the commitment to human creativity and the explosion of apprehensions of 'what must be'. Consequently, the conflict of contemporary life runs through sociology itself, threatening it with dissolution. On the one hand reason can crush the human, and on the other human creativity can deny reason. It is the Borgesian dialectic. Both alternatives point to a kind of meaninglessness if they are not pulled together. In this way Bauman identified a chance for the salvation of the promise of each. It can be achieved through the calling of sociology to occupy the middle ground between reason and creativity. A long quotation makes the point very clearly. Using terminology which is extremely anachronistic given his subsequent work, but outlining a position from which he has never substantially departed, Bauman said:

> In this critical turning point in the history of civilization, sociology, the one area of human intellectual endeavour which can bridge the gap between cultural and natural, subjective and objective, art and science, has a crucially important function to perform. It must strive to re-marry masses and reason, human life and rationality, humanity and efficiency – the couples whom modern civilization separated and whose divorce the learned priests of this civilization have sanctified.[29]

He said, 'our vocation, after all these unromantic years, may become again a test-field of courage, consistency, and loyalty to human values'.[30] Bauman's position was one stressing how sociology as a vocation may become a way of withstanding science evacuating all values from the world, and the fashions of unmoored creativity destroying everything reason has bequeathed to it. It is about the embrace of possibility whilst knowing that possibilities can only be glimpsed in the circumstances of their evident impossibility. Leszek Kołakowski once put the conundrum very neatly, albeit in a different context, when he announced: 'the impossible at a given moment can become possible only by being stated at a time when it is impossible'.[31] Consequently this is no escape from the world; rather it is confrontation with it. For the sociologist this means a determination to stand in the middle which is ambivalently situated between the necessary and the possible, withstanding assault from all directions, yet saved by a sense of vocation making him or her do it again and again.

Indeed the vocation needs to be reaffirmed continuously. As Bauman said when talking about his teachers, Stanisław Ossowski and Julian Hochfeld: 'What I learned from them was that sociology has no other – and cannot have any other – sense ... than of an ongoing commentary on human "lived experience," as transient and obsessively self-updating as that experience itself'.[32] The work consequently never ceases, one's understanding is never complete, and one must have the humility to return day after day. Similarly Bergman said one must always hold one's communion. It is not enough to have held communion once or, indeed, to refuse to hold it because of more personal considerations. It is not good enough to have held communion *yesterday* because today requires its own actions. Tomas Ericsson held communion regardless of his illness and was saved, and a parallel theme can be found in Bauman. Vocations, he said, are not a 'one-off feat. Vocations, unlike other pastimes, tend to be lifelong.'[33] Commitment to a vocation therefore makes it possible for life to be saved from the blasts of transient *experiences* through the iron of cumulative *experience*. Vocation is about Benjamin's *Erfahrung* and a repudiation of what he called *Erlbenis*.[34] The vocational principle of always holding one's communion makes it possible for life to be a demanding confrontation with the fate of the times.

It is completely beside the point whether anyone is in the congregation to hear the words to which they are invited to listen. The vocation demands one always holds one's communion, and if the calling has been upheld today that is as much as it is possible to ask. At least today the vocation has been reasserted and there has been a statement of the possibility of salvation from the times. In this way a commitment has been made to be for the other. Just as a religious service is held for the congregation, a book is written for its readers. Yet whether or not anyone comes to these communions is their decision to make. All Tomas Ericsson and Zygmunt Bauman can do is extend to others the possibility of receiving the communion they continue to offer.

Notes

* I would like to thank Kieran Flanagan for his helpful comments on an earlier version of this essay.

1 Janina Bauman, *A Dream of Belonging: My Years in Postwar Poland* (London: Virago, 1988), 67.

2 *A Dream of Belonging*, 85.

3 Zygmunt Bauman, *Modernity and Ambivalence* (Cambridge: Polity, 1991), 238–45.

4 Zygmunt Bauman, *Life in Fragments: Essays in Postmodern Morality* (Oxford: Blackwell, 1995), 270.

5 Zygmunt Bauman, *Liquid Modernity* (Cambridge: Polity, 2000), 84.

6 Zygmunt Bauman, *Liquid Love* (Cambridge: Polity, 2003), 81–5.

7 Zygmunt Bauman and Citlali Rovirosa-Madrazo, *Living on Borrowed Time* (Cambridge: Polity, 2010), 158.

8 Zygmunt Bauman, *44 Letters from the Liquid Modern World* (Cambridge: Polity, 2010), 153–6.

9 Zygmunt Bauman, Michael Hviid Jacobsen and Keith Tester, *What Use Is Sociology?* (Cambridge: Polity, 2013), 63–5.

10 Zygmunt Bauman, *Thinking Sociologically* (Oxford: Blackwell, 1990), 179.

11 Peter Beilharz, *Zygmunt Bauman: Dialectic of Modernity* (London: Sage, 2000).

12 Zygmunt Bauman and Keith Tester, *Conversations with Zygmunt Bauman* (Cambridge: Polity, 2001), 24.

13 Jorge Luis Borges, *Labyrinths: Selected Stories and Other Writings* (Harmondsworth: Penguin, 1970), 51.

14 Zygmunt Bauman, *Culture as Praxis* (London: Routledge & Kegan Paul, 1973).

15 This note is *my* interpretation of why *Winter Light* is important to Bauman. I do not know – neither have I asked – whether or not Bauman agrees with me. In other words, beyond the initial anecdote which stimulated these reflections, this chapter operates entirely at the level of the reading of publicly available texts. It makes absolutely no claim to privileged knowledge.

16 Ingmar Bergman, *Images: My Life in Film*, trans. Marianne Ruuth (London: Faber & Faber, 1995), 245.

17 Bergman in Raphael Shargel, *Ingmar Bergman: Interviews* (Jackson: University of Mississippi Press, 2007), 75.

18 Bergman, *Images*, 257.

19 Bergman, *Images*, 265.

20 Søren Kierkegaard, *The Sickness unto Death*, trans. Alastair Hannay (Harmondsworth: Penguin, 1989).

21 Bergman, *Images*, 271.

22 Bergman in Shargel, *Ingmar Bergman*, 46.

23 Bauman, *Liquid Love*.

24 Keith Tester and Michael Hviid Jacobsen, *Bauman before Postmodernity: Invitation, Conversations and Annotated Bibliography 1953–1989* (Aalborg: Aalborg University Press, 2005).

25 Ingmar Bergman, *The Magic Lantern: An Autobiography*, trans. Joan Tate (London: Hamish Hamilton, 1988), 273.

26 Max Weber, *Gesammelte Aufsätze zur Religionssoziologie* (Tübingen: Mohr-Siebeck, 1920).

27 Max Weber, *Gesammelte Politische Schriften* (Munich: Duncker and Humblot, 1921), quoted in H.H. Gerth and C. Wright Mills (eds), *From Max Weber: Essays in Sociology* (London: Routledge & Kegan Paul, 1948), 128.

28 Max Weber, *Gesammelte Aufsätze sur Wissenschaftslehre* (Tübingen: Mohr-Siebeck, 1922), quoted in Gerth and Mills, *From Max Weber*, 155.

29 Bauman, *Culture as Praxis*, 202.

30 Bauman, *Culture as Praxis*, 203.

31 Leszek Kołakowski, *Marxism and Beyond: On Historical Understanding and Individual Responsibility*, trans. Jane Zielonko Peel (London: Paladin, 1969), 92.

32 Bauman in Bauman and Tester, *Conversations with Zygmunt Bauman*, 20.

33 Bauman in Bauman and Tester, *Conversations with Zygmunt Bauman*, 158.

34 Walter Benjamin, *Illuminations*, trans. Harry Zohn (London: Fontana, 1973).

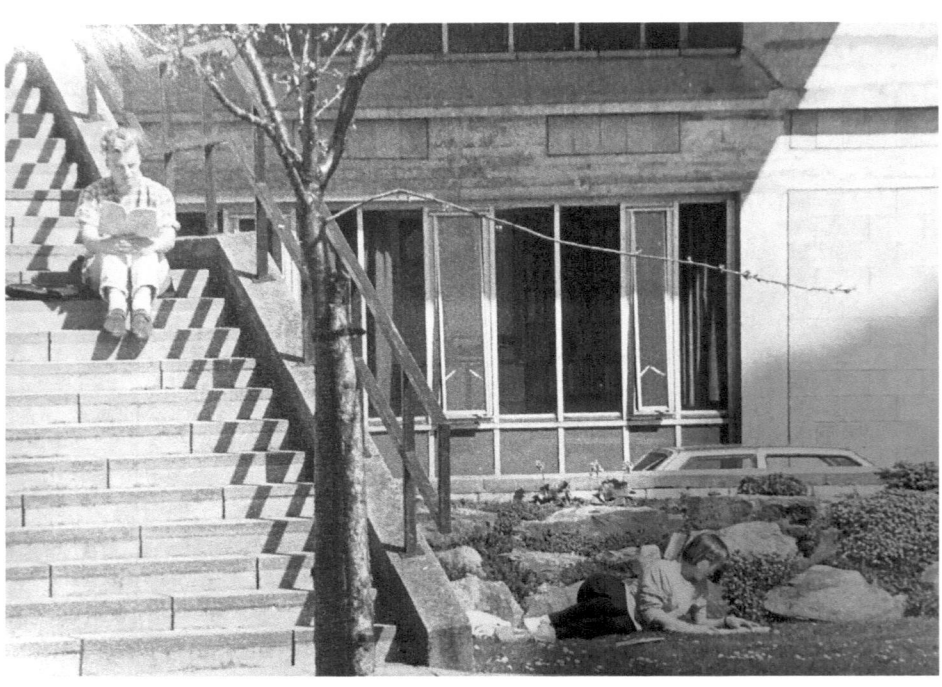

Now with the apprentice's trials and tribulations behind, boldly go where no master before dared or was allowed to!!! By the way, when will you give me a chance to celebrate at Lawnswood Gardens the beginning of another glorious life chapter?

Even an invitation to tea was charged with the linguistic flair and trademark verbosity of Zygmunt's prose. Prior to my first visit I recall not really knowing what sociology was, and wondered what we'd talk about. I soon came to learn that Zygmunt was not only a Jack of all trades but a master of many of them too, and that conversation – much like alcohol – flowed freely at Lawnswood Gardens.

No topic was off limits, Zygmunt's polymathic mind equally at home analysing football, Faust, and everything in between. But what united these myriad topics was that, in conversation, Zygmunt embellished his speech with quotes, metaphors, analogies and idioms. My favourite, and oft-recited on our visits, was: 'there is a time for fishing and a time for mending the nets'. I was never quite sure which we were supposed to be doing.

Frequently, Zygmunt would stride off post-conversation and return with a book – or multiple books – related to a topic we'd been discussing. Seldom did we leave empty-handed and he would never hear of them being returned. Only once was I able to reciprocate, giving Zygmunt a copy of Jean Giono's *The Man Who Planted Trees*. When I saw him the next day I was greeted with an enthusiastic review and enquiries as to how I'd come across it. Such was the voracity of his own appetite for books and fondness for trees, he'd read it immediately.

The books at Lawnswood Gardens had a magical quality, seeming to multiply at will like something out of a Borges story. How to solve the problem of ever-growing volumes of books? Build your own shelves out of bricks and boards. I spent every visit marvelling not only at the books themselves but the structural masterpieces that were Zygmunt's shelves. The two existed in symbiosis – I was never actually sure whether the shelves held the books or vice versa.

Much like the spontaneous order those shelves provided amidst the chaos, books themselves are a lens through which we can view the complex world and gain a sense of order. Both through his own writing and through books that he opened my eyes to, Zygmunt changed my view of the world.

Grandparents are important role models in life, as well as mentors, cooks, secret-keepers and storytellers. Zygmunt fulfilled many of these roles, and Lawnswood Gardens was a welcome retreat. The grandmother-in-law I never met, I got to know through her own books – also shedding faint light on the past of the Zygmunt I knew in the present.

To me Zygmunt was, is, and always will be, immortalised in books. On his passing many of the books that belonged to him now sit on our shelves, so that he lives on, if you will, in papertuity ...

Ben Hepworth

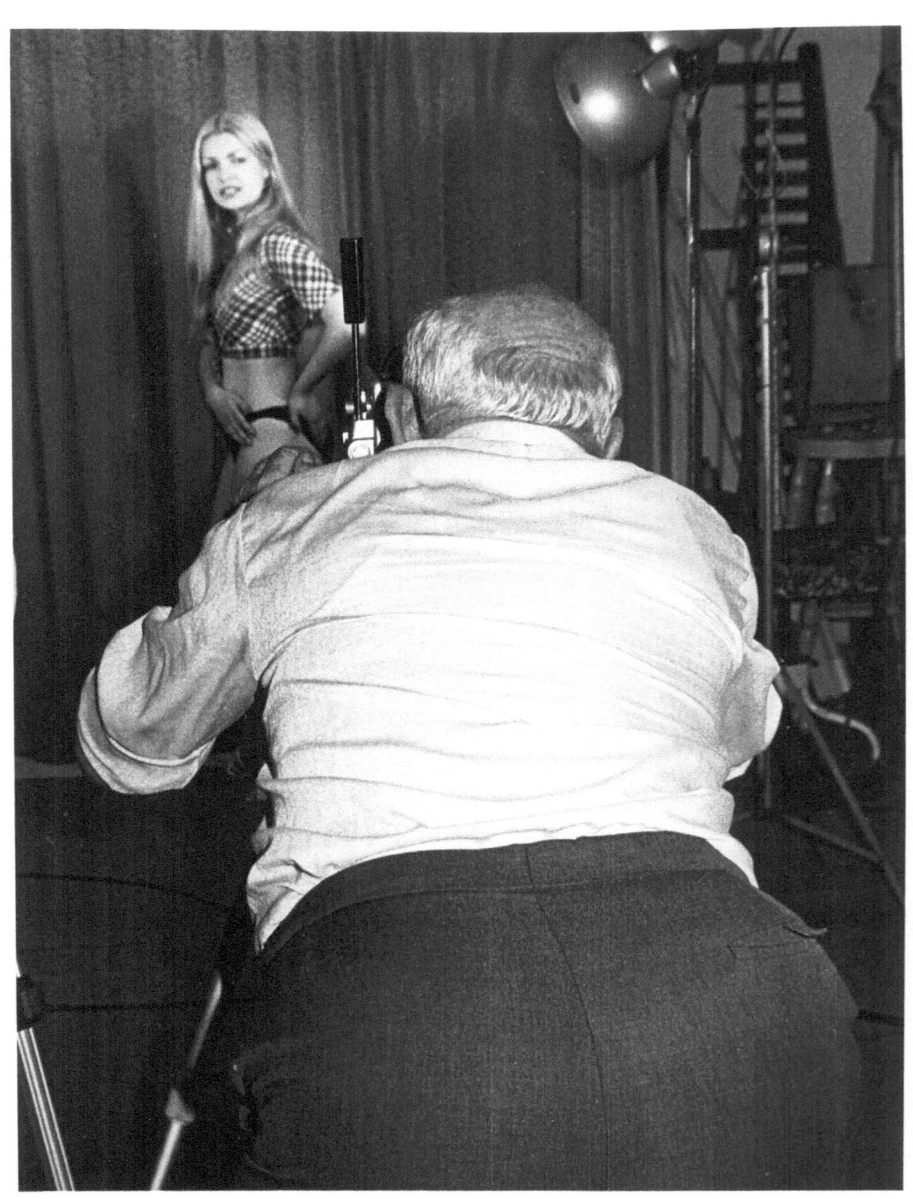

Bent double, shirt wrinkled, trousers taut enough to reveal their stitching, the hero of this image is not the person who turned up to the studio that day expecting to be a subject. Like the ambushed studio photographer, my grandfather probably didn't expect one day to become the subject of this photograph either. Such is the purpose of this book, however, and my job as the image's narrator. Now, standing at the back of this slowly lengthening queue of watched watchers, I must decide what kind of subject *I* want to be in trying to understand the image.

Should I play the academic; a difficult lens to resist when trying to think about my grandfather's view of the world? In the photograph's backstage optic, I might recognise his fascination with the hidden (and often unsavoury) infrastructures that underpin society's most visible headline moments, whether it's the Holocaust or fast fashion. I could talk about the ambiguity of the scene (is it a portrait to be cherished by a loved one forever? Or another disposable advertisement feeding capitalism's churning appetite for new material?) and how it typifies the changing status of art in a liquid modern world?

Or should I play the photographer; a passion we shared, though never at the same time? I could comment on the clever use of the 'frames within frames' trope; not actually visible in the image but implied through concentric points of view. While the woman's hands frame a slender physique, Bauman uses his lens's distortion to accentuate the man's natural pear-shape. Against the soft-edged studio lighting that flatters the model, a harsh and primitive flashgun irons wrinkles into full-blown creases and lends an overall guerrilla-style spontaneity to the image's aesthetic. I could admire these strategic uses of technique and contrast to ascribe retroactive deliberateness or even genius, as critics so often do.

Yes, unlike the two photographers and three models I have before me, I get to choose what kind of subject I want to be. Despite this, I feel most compelled (indeed qualified) to read this image as a grandson. Compared to more premeditated intellectual or artistic instincts, I recognise here the boyish humour of the man perched at the corner of the kitchen table. In that setting, amusing stories from my student life used to delight my grandfather infinitely more than the jargon-riddled ramblings of my undergraduate essays. Engaging anecdotes, visual metaphors, a good joke, so often the tools of his own teaching, seemed always to light up his eyes more than the dizzying intellect of an earnest acolyte could. It's this love of elegant narratives, and above all informality, that ties this photograph to my grandfather – a man who produced clever things in pursuit of simple ends.

So, while academic and technical prowess may feature in this photographic hall of mirrors, they do so like the made-up model; as the celebrity sideshow relegated to the corner of the frame. It's the spontaneous and irreverent impulses of my grandfather, collecting a story, that take the spotlight.

Karl Dudman

Gazing sociologically, thinking photographically, deciphering gender

Antony Bryant and Griselda Pollock

Zygmunt Bauman was not privy to feminist or social-historical theories of the photographic image or cinema during the 1970–80s. To him as photographer and sociologist, theories of the gaze – as surveillance, as imposing a burden of representation, as articulating a phallocentric psycho-sexual scopic regime shaped erotically by fetishism and trading in sadistic voyeurism, or as plotting out queer fields of desire – were alien, unknown and unacknowledged.[1] Bauman entered photography through the strongly masculine community of amateur photographers seeking mastery of a chemical craft and the technical knowhow to rival the great photographers and their choices. Amateur photographers repeated faithfully the museum-established genres of historical photography for valuing photography alongside the visual arts such as a focus on author/ artist, period, style, iconography and the genres of landscape, the portrait, and the nude (primarily the female nude). History painting, the most revered amongst the fine arts of painting, was replaced, in photography, by documentary. Moreover, serious photography – involving specialist equipment, darkroom, developer and baths for chemicals in which images were developed and fixed – was expensive. There is, indeed, a history of women in photography, for instance, Lady Clementina Hawarden (1822–65) and Julia Margaret Cameron (1815–79) right through all the movements in photography in the twentieth century. As amateurs, however, it was men who typically owned cameras and made photography their hobby; so Bauman learned his craft in the world of men with their gear and chemistry, insulated from critical perspectives on the semiotics of the power, as much as the sexual politics, of the gaze. It is this 'paradox' that enables us to analyse the place of photographs by Zygmunt Bauman lodged in our domestic space.

In our home, we live surrounded by photographs. Our children's lives have been captured, along with their interactions with their paternal grandparents

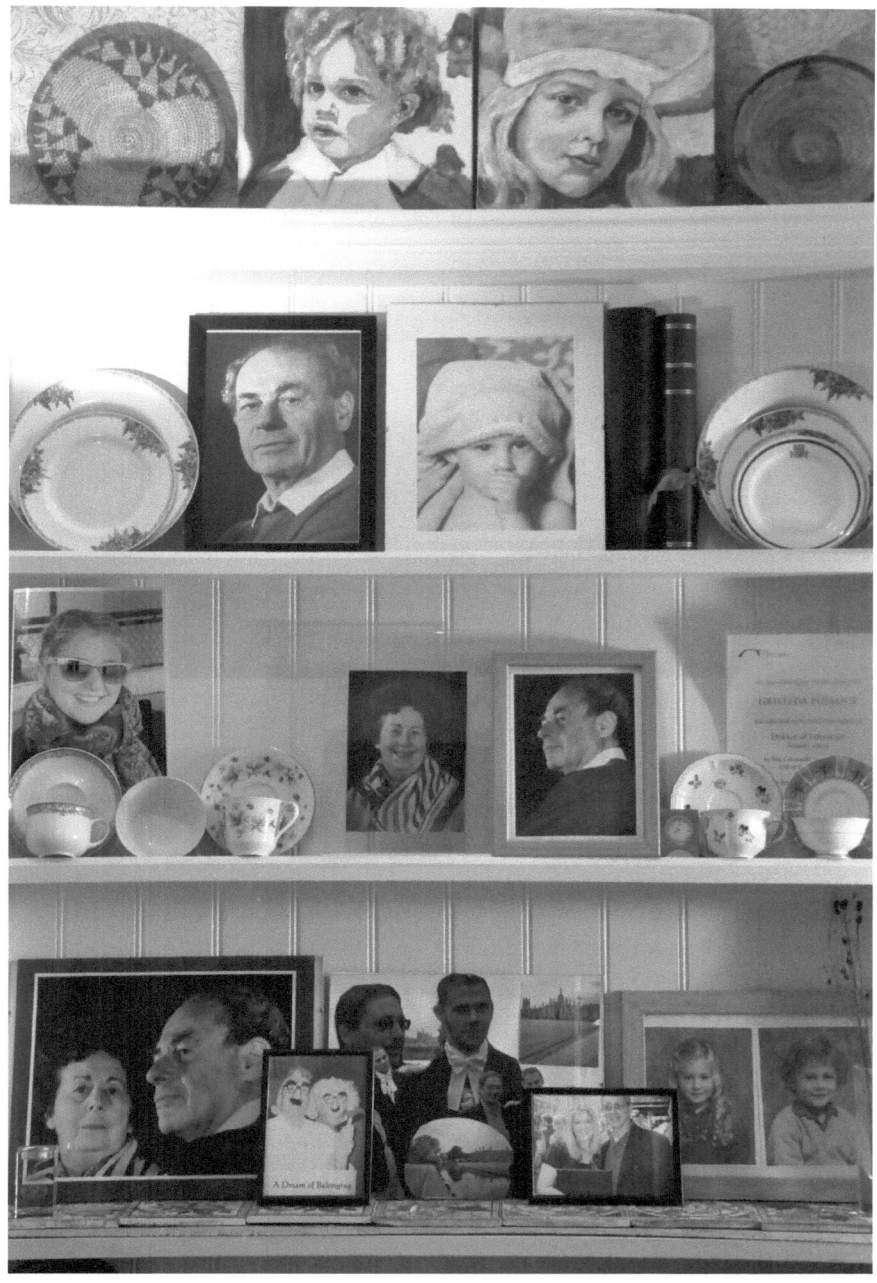

(neither Griselda's mother nor her father survived into their lives). The colour snaps are punctuated by framed, black-and-white, posed photographic portraits by Zygmunt Bauman – of Tony's parents – Paul and Leonie Bryant – and several of Griselda as a young woman, as a pregnant woman, and as mother with her daughter. Their difference lies not only in being black-and-white analogue photographs of posed subjects versus casual colour snaps. They open on to the sociological and symbolic freight in photography that the theorist Julia Hirsch in *Family Photographs* and the artist Jo Spence in *Beyond the Family Album* analysed by 'reading' the family album.[2]

In 1980, Julia Hirsch was one of the first scholars to situate photographs of the family within the longer history of image-making, notably across Western art, and to identify, thereby, the complex roles of photography in relation to the construction of the family as an idea and an ideology.

> The authority of these conventions, like the hold of traditional family roles which makes us want strong fathers and nurturing mothers, living children and sheltering homes is difficult to resist. Professional as well as amateur photographers still place families in poses that express and cater to these longings. Family photography is an aesthetic, social and moral product of which the family is at once the seller and consumer.[3]

Unsaid, but operative, concepts of gender and formations of class and race produce a social unit of both physical reproduction and social labour of its reproduction. Differentiations of men and women, suppressed intimations of sexualities, variations of security and precarity are inscribed by representation shaped by the historical forms of the family that is both the object and the prime consumer of such imaging that is always more than a mere record. Hirsch explains:

> The editorial authority is exercised as well whenever we take family photographs. There is always a moment in the present that beckons to immortality, that moment that is not only felt but immediately seen as its own past and second-hand future … Lumps of experience, rites of passage, grains of poignancy and promise: all of these turn us into artists sorting through life in search of shapes and events which our cameras will turn into symbols or allegories. The sleeping child, the fleshy mother, the tired father, the testy siblings can, in the quick eye of the camera, be transformed into images of innocence, protectiveness, enterprise and sharing. Family photography is not only an accessory to our deepest longings and regrets; it is also a set of visual rules that shape our experience and our memory.[4]

It is hard to resist this transformation of the quotidian into allegory and symbol because taking or making a photograph is an act, a practice, a search for an image, none of which is given by what is before the camera or through the clicking the shutter. Hirsch attributes to the camera a transformative, not a documentary, function. What photographic practice yields responds to what it is that we, collectively and between photographer and photographed, yearn to grasp as hitherto unarticulated 'longings and regrets', namely *affects*. Yet the iteration across iconographic traditions already waiting to affirm the quality of any one photograph as an *image* contributes to an ideological script forming us as selves, gendered, sexualised, raced, classed, ageing, historical.

Hirsch's analysis coincided with the practice-based analytical work by the British working-class feminist artist Jo Spence (1934–92) in her multi-panelled photographic project *Beyond the Family Album* (1978–79).[5] Produced by the Photography Workshop, *Beyond the Family Album* is a series of ten panels in which Spence alternates autobiographical texts, personal photographs and press clippings that track the traumatic events often omitted from family photo albums – deaths, divorces, conflicts, abuse and illness. Spence removed the barrier between idealised private uses of photography in family albums and the not-so-visible ideological meanings rising to the allegorical. She also exposed the absence of the repressed by her analysis of 'visual constructions' of class and gender in the family image world that shape and iterate the social fictions of personal identities across class, race and gender.[6] One absence is the father, usually taking the picture.

In our domestic display, there are individual and combined portraits of a couple.

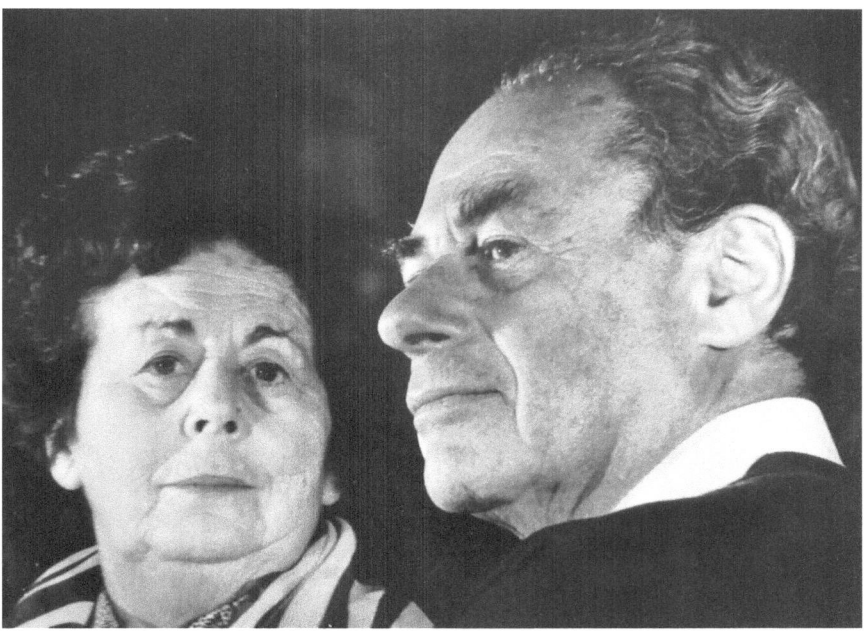

Such titling opens on to Hirsch's allegorical reading. The photos show an older couple who have lived long lives side-by-side. Are they providing a portrait of a marriage? Possibly. Yet Bauman's photograph situates the two people in space without the conventions of the marital couple. He juxtaposes two faces, creating disjunction through the different pathways of each gaze. Both turn their gazes inwards, almost in a moment of reverie that implies a past.

Bauman photographed several couples. What a few of his personally invited sitters shared with him in terms of pasts and presents, however, was exile, forced migration, displacement, foreignness – lost pasts. The conditions of such loss were traumatic and historical. In this case, there is a story to be told which comes later in this chapter. Others in this volume, with similar histories of escape, exile, grief, mourning and losses of displaced and bereaved European Jewish parents, may also have shared their own sense that such portraits of elderly, Continental Jewish couples are a critical and aesthetically charged archive (see the portrait of John Schwarzmantel's parents chosen by Janet Wolff, p. 90 above) that mirrors obliquely the singular history of forced exile of survivors Zygmunt and Janina Bauman. In her recent sociological analysis of the formation of Zygmunt Bauman as an intellectual, Izabela Wagner traces the multiple displacements and experienced outsiderness in the trajectory of Zygmunt's life that, she argues, affectively lined and sociologically directed the trajectory of his thought.[7] The reverie, requested by the photographer or assumed by the sitters, becomes less an oblique index of the conventions of family photography than an affecting signifier of a deeper – and shared – sense of loss and disconnection. The faces loom out of darkness and hover in space.

Their stories, and others like them from Bauman's Jewish sitters, move the 'family' or 'couple' image on to the plane of history. These are the faces of those few who 'survived' to have their lives reshaped as the remnant of the European Jewish worlds, Western and Eastern, destroyed by fascist genocide now termed the Shoah or Holocaust. They were violently expelled from the lives they were meant to have lived, many the only survivors of entire families, forced to inhabit an unfamiliar culture in which their European Jewishness was as alien to local British Jewish populations as their traumas of loss were illegible. They were, moreover, divided from their children growing up as part of British culture. Belonging to what has come to be theorised as a 'second generation' – unknowing inheritors of parental trauma often 'transmitted' through parental silence about their pasts – such children became, however, unconscious witnesses to the unspoken losses of their parents and unknowing inheritors of unsayable traumas.[8] The children's lives were suspended between an encrypted and lost world carried by their parents and the local cultural world which they inhabited in a Britain that did not fully know or comprehend the

Continental Jewish world of their parents. The photographs of the parents of some of his colleagues at the University of Leeds such as John Schwarzmantel and Antony Bryant were mirrors of Zygmunt's and Janina's experiences – despite differences because of the delayed experience of expulsion and forced migration in the case of the Bauman family. Yet, we are suggesting, the studies of their parents can also be read obliquely as indirect explorations of Janet Wolff, John Schwarzmantel and Antony Bryant, Zygmunt Bauman's younger associates in a sociological enterprise, who are, as second generation, also historical-sociological entities. Of this younger trio with common experience of refugee-exile parents, only Janet Wolff was photographed.

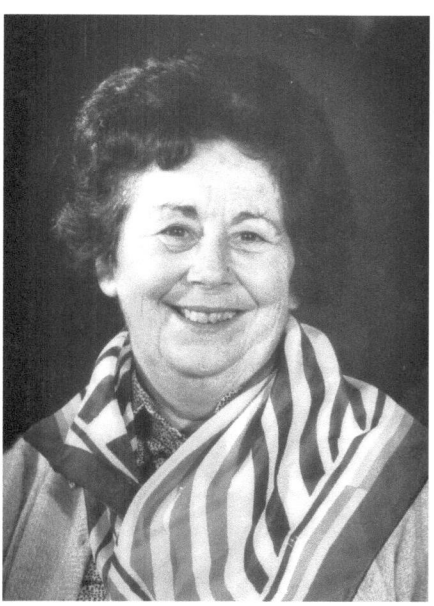 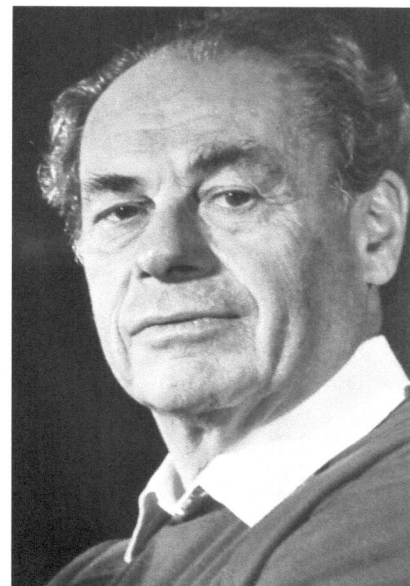

Zygmunt Bauman also individually photographed Leonie Bryant, née Magnus, born in Berlin in 1917 and Paul Bryant, né Pawel Blumenzweig, born in Teplitz, then Czechoslovakia, in 1913. The shadowing by trauma yields to the force of gender typing. Leonie Bryant smiles pleasingly within a photographic space that frames and contains her look as it is being viewed by the photographer. Paul Bryant does not engage with his photographer. He looks down in this close-cropped image that endows his unsmiling face with both a sombre authority and a sad grandeur as it emerges from its dark ground.

Femininity is a convention – the smile – while masculinity appears singular, if equally inscribed by well-defined differentiating codes. Bauman photographed Griselda Pollock – topic, author and analyst in this context.

Taking their place within the genre of portraiture, we have a trio of closely framed images of her face. One shows its subject in side-view with eyes downcast – is there a troubling touch of 'Princess Di' reticence and bad hairstyle? A second presents a frontal image with the same face, eyes open and with a steady gaze creating both a strong self-presence and an element of knowing encounter with the photographing gaze. The third image uses a wider lens while coming closer to the first image. The face is in three-quarter profile and, frankly, the gaze seems empty, stilted and over-posed.

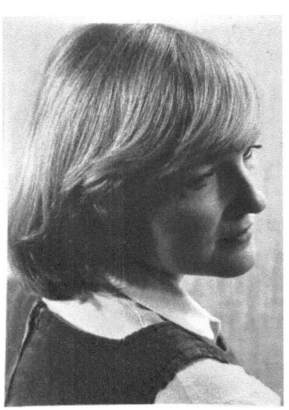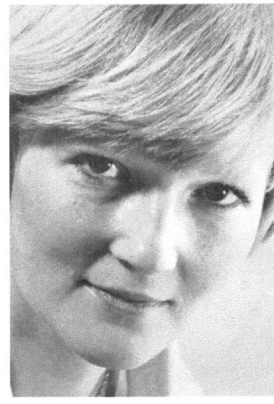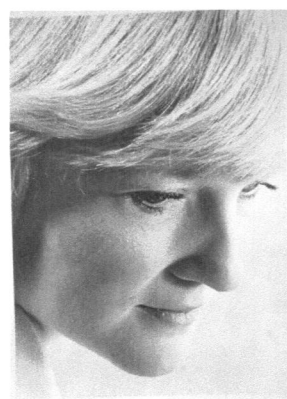

The photograph does, however, carry incidental and entirely personal signification. We can recognise the clothes. In the first, Griselda is wearing a corduroy maternity dress that dates this image to the later stages of her first pregnancy in 1983. Using Julia Hirsch's analysis, the choice of model for these images moves from the anecdotal – they came to tea and she was invited upstairs to be photographed, a willing party to Zygmunt's new hobby – to the question: were the poses intended to be expressive of the idea of expectancy and maternal femininity? While familiars of the Bauman intellectual-social community were invited to indulge their host by offering themselves to his camera, there cannot but be a sociological dimension that frames the aesthetic project. Bauman was photographing a young woman but also a mature feminist academic on the cusp of having a child, fulfilling – in conventional terms – her 'proper' destiny by suspending her immediate working career. This suspicion is further supported by the fact that Zygmunt Bauman did say to Griselda, on visiting after this birth, and with some regret: 'it is a pity, you *would have been* a significant art historian'. Did he really think that having a child inevitably spelled the end or even just a derailment of her career in unpaid motherhood? Unlikely, since his own family history in postwar Poland included both socialist-imposed gender equality in terms of working for the new state and a personal history in so far as Janina Bauman worked throughout her motherhood that included having a daughter followed by twins. Reality and ideology sometimes fail to correspond.

Griselda has written elsewhere that she is entirely grateful to Zygmunt for his comment – serious or ironic – that motherhood would end or interrupt her intellectual career.[9] She never reproached him because ironically it fired her feminist determination to prove him wrong by maintaining a highly productive intellectual life even as she cared for her child[ren].

A solitary photograph in our collection dates a moment late in Griselda's second pregnancy in 1985–86. Gone is the Di haircut, replaced by boldly short hair framing her face in a frontal pose. Griselda recalls the shocking decision to make this change defiantly disconnecting her advanced pregnant state – indicative of conventions of maternal femininity – from its typical signifiers. Perhaps this radical disjuncture prompted another sitting during a social visit to the Bauman residence. In the steady gaze, we might read a calm defiance or discern a slightly quizzical curl to the lips, an expression hovering between proper seriousness for the business of being photographed and the memory per-haps of the photographer's expressed regret at a wasted intellectual career while she enumerates in her head some of her numerous publications in a sustained combination of parenting, teaching and writing.

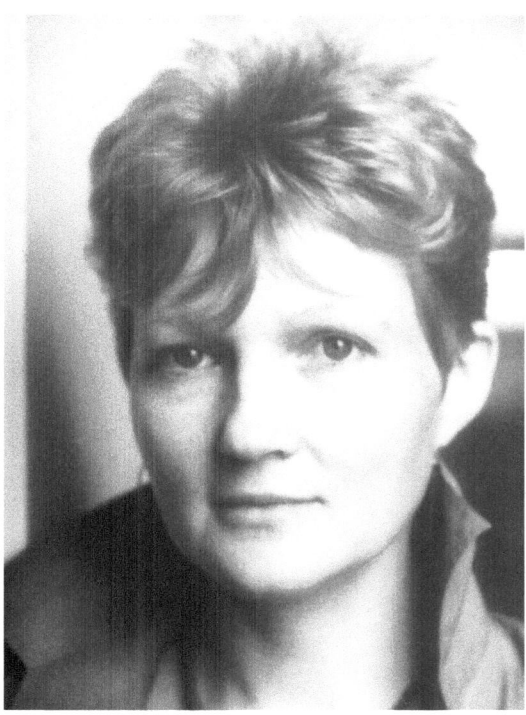

A final visit to the Bauman studio returns us to the territory of Julia Hirsch once more. A series of informal images were made of Griselda and our daughter Hester (b. 1986). This image is all about hair. It was, sadly, the era of the mullet, while also capturing the glorious golden curls of the little girl whose disdain for the formal process of posing – or perhaps her childish innocence of the protocols of posing femininity for the gaze of others – expresses itself in using an indecipherable toy as a kind of flute. Or perhaps she is merely indulging in childish orality with whatever was to hand. Yet she is looking at the photographer with quiet intent. Griselda's face settles now in conventional feminine self-presentation. Aligned with the portrait-mode in the photograph of Leonie Bryant, Griselda's face is open, half smiling. She was, perhaps, chatting and this allows for animation in lieu of pose.

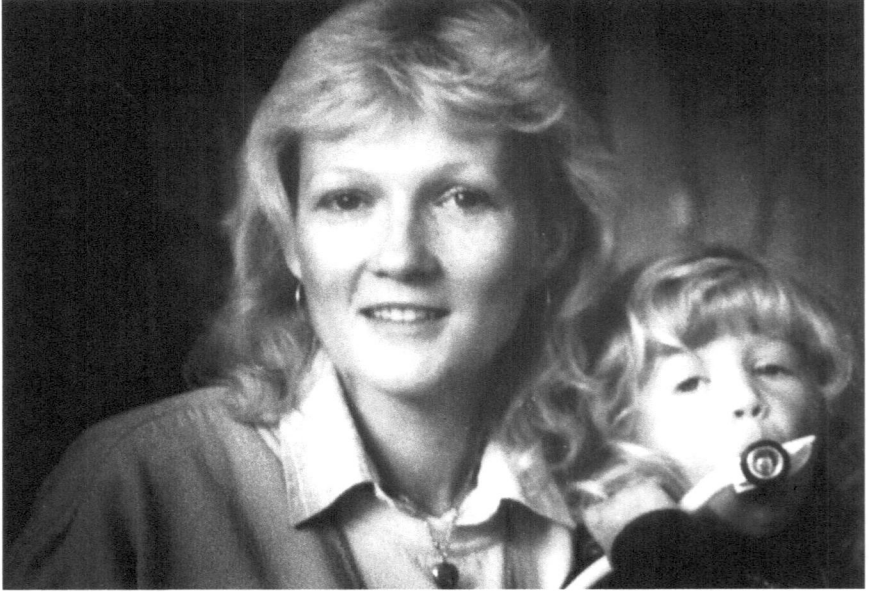

From this survey of Bauman's photographic presence in our home emerges a telling absence. There are no corresponding photographs of Antony [Tony] Bryant. Why was *he* not invited upstairs to perform – in Hirsch's terms – an allegorical image of the 'young intellectual', 'the budding sociologist', 'a young father' or 'the British-born son of Continental refugees'? What made Bauman interested in women or couples as subjects, and not younger men? We cannot answer a question that, nevertheless, needs to be posed in terms of a focus on gender in Bauman's photographic practice. Now, therefore, we need the story of how it was that Antony Bryant, his parents and his young family encountered

Zygmunt Bauman and joined a special group of exiles of many kinds clustered in Leeds, in sociology and related social art historical and cultural analysis and came under his photographic gaze.

Tony first encountered Zygmunt fleetingly, when he went to Leeds to be interviewed for a one-year post in his Department of Sociology some time in early 1978. Having been appointed to the post, he moved to Leeds in September 1978 and so began a friendship, personal and intellectual, with Zygmunt that lasted for almost forty years. Soon after starting in his department Zygmunt and Janina invited Tony for lunch the following Saturday; 'please arrive by 12.00'. Colleagues warned him not to plan anything else that day, as 'lunch' would last well into the afternoon or early evening. The food would be Polish and lavish, the amount only exceeded by volume of alcohol, and so it proved to be on all counts.

Zygmunt quizzed Tony about his background. He was particularly interested when told that Tony's parents were both refugees. Tony's father had fled from what was then Czechoslovakia soon after the German invasion in 1938, attempting to make it to Britain overland and being turned back at the Belgian border on the eve of the outbreak of war. Forced to recross Germany in a sealed train, he failed to persuade his parents to escape with him eastwards. Alone, he risked the dangerous journey by boat down the Danube arriving eventually in British Palestine where he was promptly imprisoned by the British. He escaped to join the Free Czech Army assembling on the Southern French coast at Aigues Mortes, arriving finally in England in 1939 under that 'flag' only to be immediately detained because of his known left-wing politics. Benefiting from fluency in French and English, he became an invaluable mediator for his fellows who were, of course, interned as 'aliens' in various racecourses (including York) and other sites before being invited to join the British Army. The Army suggested that he change his evidently Jewish surname Blumenzweig (*Branch of Flowers*). He chose the anodyne English *Bryant*, picked out from the box of matches used to light his cigarettes – Bryant & May – having also been advised by the Army officers to select a name beginning with the first letter of his original surname. Recruited and promised by the British 'as an officer and a gentleman' that he and his colleagues would fight the war in Europe, he was dispatched initially to recruit more soldiers from the colonised countries on the West Coast of Africa before being deployed with them to Burma. He returned to Britain in 1946.

Tony's mother had escaped from Berlin in 1936, together with her mother and an uncle, because her dentist brother had been able to set himself up in London a few years earlier through the assistance of a British dentist he had encountered at an international medical conference in London in 1932. The latter, hearing of the anti-Jewish persecution in Germany after 1933, had immediately reached out to assist this casual acquaintance. A trained infant teacher,

Leonie first worked as a domestic and then as a nanny, the sculptor Jacob Epstein being one of her early employers.

Having learnt some of this, Zygmunt instructed Tony in no uncertain terms: 'When they come to visit, you *must* tell me so that we can invite them for lunch'. A few weeks later the three Bryants arrived for lunch – 12.00 prompt. Tony had duly passed on the warning about the alcohol, and, as he was the driver, attempted – not entirely successfully – to limit his intake. At the time Zygmunt's hobby was not photography but wine-making; he was also a keen gardener. All three were plied not only with various spirits and wines from the off-licence but also with tastings of various vintages of *Château Bauman* – the final one being *Baumagnac*, Zygmunt's homebrew version of Armagnac. Relating this later to a colleague, Tony was told that there was no higher accolade, as it was reserved for special occasions and special people.

Near the end of the academic year 1978–79, the University of Leeds planned to hold its first Open Day. This was announced at the monthly Sociology departmental meeting. These meetings were nothing like those described in Malcolm Bradbury's *The History Man*, although it was reputed that the minutes for several meetings included the phrase 'At this point a Polish joke was told'. For some departments, such as Medicine or Physics, the issue of what to do for Open Day was fairly straightforward; but how should Sociology respond? Tony was a keen photographer, proud owner of an iconic Asahi Pentax. Most of his photos were taken in black-and-white, using fast film and various filters. Some of these photos adorned his office and colleagues had commented on them, and perhaps they contributed to the plan to make and show shots of various Leeds locations with text explaining that sociology was the study of where and how people lived, their interactions and interrelationships.

Zygmunt showed a keen interest in the photos, and the exhibit clearly sparked an interest that made him jettison wine-making and gardening. In fact, it was probably at this point – 1979 – that he ceased any gardening. Thus, in his later years, as one battled one's way from the gate to the house through the ever-expanding undergrowth, Zygmunt would explain that 'Darwin is my gardener'. Zygmunt rapidly moved from simply taking photos to developing them himself, joining a camera club and winning many competitions. He set up a rudimentary darkroom, and soon began to mix his own chemicals for developing and fixing, being dissatisfied with the ready-made versions. Having mastered many of the technical complexities of photography, and won several local prizes, Zygmunt ceased as abruptly as he had begun.

Bauman was a distinguished as well as an accomplished photographer. In our short piece in this volume (pp. 26–7), we wrote about the sociological gaze that we can read in his choice of topics and scenes. In this longer essay, we focus on a social relationship with the photographer turning our sociological

and cultural analytical gazes back on his work. Not only are the Bauman photographs in our home precious portraits of beloved but deceased parents or
grandparents who gaze down on or smile at us (now also in our sixties and
seventies), they are also historic portraits bearing indirect witness to shared
traumatic experience, particular to each refugee or exile.

Since Zygmunt Bauman took up photography in the late 1970s, the study
and commemoration of the Holocaust – to which Zygmunt made such a profound contribution in his book *Modernity and the Holocaust* (1989) – has been joined
by testimony to the condition known as 'second generation' introduced above.[10]
This is an acknowledgement of the inherited, often unrecognised, affects carried
by those born into families shattered, displaced and bereaved by the horror they
physically but never psychologically escaped.[11] Psychoanalytical recognition of
inherited or intergenerationally transmitted trauma has been expanded by literary works, visual art and film.[12] Inspired by Zygmunt Bauman's book, following
a Cultural Studies initiative taught by Bryan Cheyette and Max Silverman for
the MA in Cultural Studies in 1989 at Leeds, in 1995 Griselda devised, and for
fifteen years taught, in an art history or fine art context, one of the first and still
one of the very few courses or modules on the formation and complexity of
the Holocaust in cultural memory and the politics of its representation across
cultural forms from art, literature, film and museums: *From Trauma to Cultural
Memory: The Unfinished Business of the Representation of the Holocaust*. The ramifica-
tions of transgenerationally transmitted trauma are also a focus topic of her
research, as is the larger field of trauma studied through a psychoanalytical
lens and by close readings of artworks produced within, and seeking to work
through, this impact of trauma, unshared, never articulated or expressed by
parents.[13]

The portraits that Zygmunt made of his own contemporaries who were the
parents of the 'second generation', therefore, are not only poignant images of
shared experience as the displaced, exiled, refugee or survivor. They are historical documents that trace the trauma of the Shoah into the subtle web of meanings that Julia Hirsch analysed as 'family photography'. Daily, we look at the
photographs around us and ask what was Zygmunt trying to see or understand
in these moments of being with others who had seen, witnessed and lived both
horror and terror and now lived displaced lives in suburban Leeds or London,
in rural Yorkshire or the South of England, surrounded both by people who
could not know what they had survived and by their own children from whom
they sometimes withheld their own pasts? When you live with portraits such
as these, even as they appear to be just images of fathers and mothers (actual
and in-law), their 'other' worlds haunt these often-sombre faces. Also a child
of Holocaust survivors, the cultural and literary theorist Marianne Hirsch has
analysed the effect of the presence in homes of surviving photographs of missing

family members and their unknown life-worlds that engender an effect she terms *post-memory*.[14]

We have also read the images of Griselda – who it is important to emphasise was not a child of Holocaust survivors even as her background is that of displacement and orphaning as an immigrant: born in one country, raised in another and in two languages, now a resident and 'passing' foreigner in Britain – through the lens of a different history element of twentieth-century history, namely feminism – both referencing political activity in the women's movement and demonstrating women's determination to combine the pleasures of parenting with their rights to intellectual fulfilment. Bauman's sociology was never attuned to gender issues or directly cognisant of feminist sociology or cultural theory. He extended his respect, however, to the person. In his portraits of women academic colleagues and friends, and notably of the five astonishing and brilliant women in his life – Janina and Aleksandra (Ola), his daughters Anna, Irena and Lydia – and their daughters, he was creating images of such respect as well as of affection and a very vital element of his life, friendship. Zygmunt Bauman excelled in all three. The photos in our house keep his and Janina's worlds present in ours through his having created for posterity not only aesthetically impressive, but also, as we have argued, socio-historically telling portraits of people marked by one of *the* events of the twentieth century that Bauman the sociologist made us rethink – the Holocaust. His images can be read through a triple lens of compassion, critical analysis and respect.

Notes

1 Classic texts include John Berger, *Ways of Seeing* (Harmondsworth: Penguin, 1982); Laura Mulvey, 'Visual Pleasure and Narrative Cinema', *Screen*, 16.3 (1975), 6–18; Victor Burgin, *Thinking Photography* (Basingstoke: Palgrave Macmillan, 1982); John Tagg, *The Burden of Representation: Essays on Photographies and Histories* (Basingstoke: Palgrave Macmillan, 1988).

2 Julia Hirsch, *Family Photographs: Content, Meaning and Effect* (Oxford: Oxford University Press, 1980).

3 Hirsch, *Family Photographs*, 13.

4 Hirsch, *Family Photographs*, 13.

5 *Beyond the Family Album* is a multi-element photographic installation that was exhibited in Paul Hill, Angela Kelly and John Tagg, *Three Perspectives in Photography: Recent British Photography* (London: Hayward Gallery, 1979).

6 Jo Spence, *Putting Myself in the Picture: A Political, Personal and Photographic Autobiography* (London: Camden Press, 1986); Jo Spence, *Cultural Sniping: The Art of Transgression* (London: Routledge, 1995).

7 Izabela Wagner, *Bauman: A Biography* (Cambridge: Polity, 2020). This impact of successive moments of expulsion and exile is an element of Wagner's

master-concept for understanding the historically and psycho-socially situated formation of Zygmunt Bauman as a sociologist.

8 For example: Helen Epstein, *Children of the Holocaust: Conversations with the Sons and Daughters of Survivors* (New York: G.P. Putnam, 1978); Anne Karpf, *The War After: Living with the Holocaust* (London: Heinemann, 1996); Eva Hoffman, *After Such Knowledge: A Meditation on the Aftermath of the Holocaust* (London: Secker & Warburg, 2004). The artists whose work explores transmitted trauma, about whom Griselda has written, include the painters Judith Tucker and Bracha L. Ettinger and, above all, the director Chantal Akerman. More recently, Janet Wolff's memoir *Austerity Baby* (Manchester: Manchester University Press, 2017) and Alba Arikha, *Major Minor: A Memoir* (London: Quartet Books, 2011) contribute to further elaborations of the form of the memoir and the processing of such experience.

9 Griselda Pollock, 'Liquid Culture, *The Art of Life* and Dancing with Tracey Emin: A Feminist Art Historian/Cultural Analyst's Perspective on Zygmunt Bauman's Missing Cultural Hermeneutics', *Thesis Eleven*, 156:1 (2020), 10–26.

10 Zygmunt Bauman, *Modernity and the Holocaust* (Cambridge: Polity, 1989); Jack Palmer and Dariusz Brzeziński (eds), *Revisiting Modernity and the Holocaust: Heritage, Dilemmas, Extensions* (Abingdon: Routledge, 2022).

11 Dina Wardi, *Memorial Candles: Children of the Holocaust* (London: Routledge, 1992); Special Issue: 'Transgenerational Transmission to the Second Generation', *Journal of Social Work and Social Policy in Israel*, 5–6 (1992).

12 For example, the novel by David Grossman, *See Under Love* (1986) (London: Jonathan Cape, 1990). See also Martin S. Berman and Milton E. Jucovy, *Generations of the Holocaust* (New York: Columbia University Press, 1982).

13 Griselda Pollock, *After-affects/After-images: Trauma and Aesthetic Transformation in the Virtual Feminist Museum* (Manchester: Manchester University Press, 2013).

14 Marianne Hirsch, *The Generation of Postmemory: Writing and Visual Culture after the Holocaust* (New York: Columbia University Press, 2012).

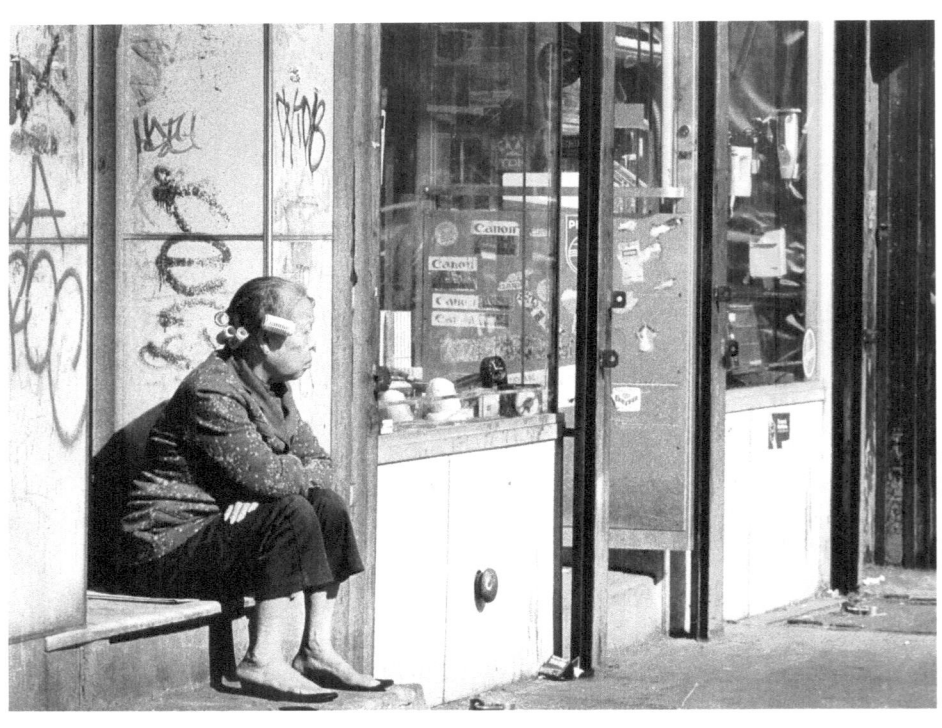

Dziadzia had his way of observing the world. For those of us lucky enough to have been his family and friends, insight was gained through long conversations in his front room. Windows overgrown with ivy (he would boast that Charles Darwin was his gardener), the little light that did enter the house was further impeded by a thick cloud of tobacco smoke and tall piles of books. Shortly after arriving you were accosted and harassed by a constant flow of food and alcohol. Conversations lasted for hours and, although filled with laughter and love, the Big Subjects of social injustice, inequality and politics were never far away.

For the rest of the world, his observations were captured in his writing or via the lens of a camera.

His writing, as we know, was profuse and became more so. He came to live by words. But in this earlier photographic period visual images had their own prominence. He left us a broad portfolio of images, unconnected, largely, to those words. So how are we to read these images? Here is a study of a subject, likely in Chinatown in Manhattan. How do we read it?

On first inspection, this photo struck me as quite sad. Contextualised by the architecture in the scene, the woman is occupying a doorway, a strange threshold between public and private for people who don't have a place to call their own. She is a solitary figure, reminding us of the individualism at the heart of capitalism. Human company conspicuously absent, she is instead surrounded by the confident, gleaming logos of large consumer brands next to which she cuts a subservient and reduced figure.

On closer inspection however, sentiment is more positive, even uplifting. Her isolation does not have to be read as loneliness. Instead, it captures someone taking time for herself, watching the world go by, enjoying the sunshine on her face. The composition of the image, placing her in the foreground, gives her a priority over those bright, crisp, corporate logos – a defiant victory for the human over the human-made.

For all the seriousness of his subject matters, *Dziadzia* was fundamentally an optimist. Anyone who ever met him will know he truly believed in the power of humanity. It's impossible to know exactly what he saw in this scene that made him reach for his camera, but I like to think it was something uplifting, rather than dispiriting.

Despite the Big Subjects, his optimism was infectious. The reason his ideas resonated with so many people worldwide was that he offered a vision of hope, not fear. After all, at the end of an evening in his company – despite being force-fed Sainsbury's spring rolls and inhaling second-hand smoke – you always left feeling better than when you arrived.

Alex Bauman-Lyons

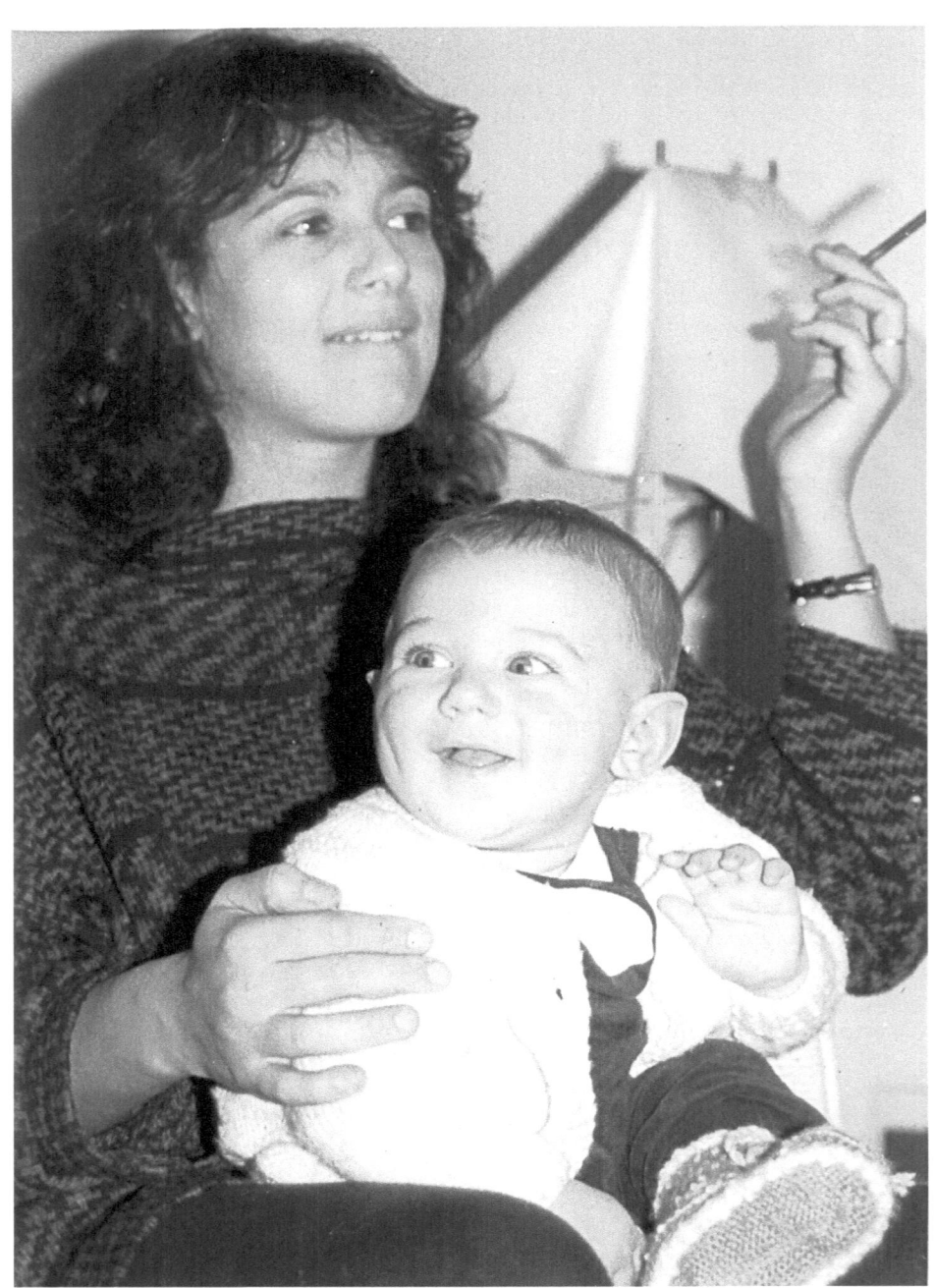

Smoking and the act of photographic snapshot, arguably, share some characteristics: both are driven by desire, both need tools of implementation and a moment in time to execute the act. Both are props to daily sorrows, special celebrations and tools of mediation within relationships. Both can be repeatedly enacted, and both can be highly annoying and intrusive to others. Both can leave us with rich recollections.

Much of my father's photography was staged in search of an insightful portrait, from the desire to capture a telling aspect of a landscape or to cast a gaze on the human condition. But when confronted with very unwilling, or even cantankerous subjects, such as his family members, he often resorted to a surreptitious snapshot.

The most fruitful conditions for such opportunistic behaviour were moments of stillness and togetherness created by our smoking ritual.

It was a ritual that a photograph could bear witness to and evoke recollection of, but could never represent in its infinite richness.

The act of smoking with my mother and father was synonymous with conversation, illuminating insights into politics and the human condition made lighter with the telling and retelling of Jewish jokes retrieved from the rich catalogue of my father's memory in intact condition.

In between cigarettes, the first one a long elegant Moore cigarette and those that followed shorter Pall Malls, we would look through new piles of books that had arrived over the week and the new clay pots made by my mother, share news of my sisters, receive gifts of movies already watched and recirculated to us with not always accurate commentary. Mixed into the conversations were details of my parents' new invitations, awards, publications and honorary doctorates exchanged with mine of the baby sleeping or not sleeping, new projects and lack of progress on the house conversion. And all the time sipping a treble Bloody Mary before noon.

Sitting down, reaching out for the offered cigarette lit by one of my father's numerous disposable lighters, leaning back in the chair and starting the conversation were the moments of continuity and conviviality and of tiny injections of happiness spanning major life events as well as the everyday. Each encounter followed by restlessness from the double stimulation of the nicotine and new understanding.

The cigarettes, which of course are very bad for us, should not be perceived in the same context as the act of smoking. At the entrance to my parents' house there was a little framed quotation: 'If you give up alcohol, cigarettes and sex, you don't live longer, it just feels like it'. Smoking was a way of living – a significant and beloved ritual I shared with my parents and the subject of this belated love letter to my parents.

'On the track leading to happiness there is no finishing line' wrote my father in *The Art of Life*. After his death it took me three years to finish smoking the remaining pack of his cigarettes and I recorded that moment in a photograph for the archive of my love.

This photograph, with others, extends the track of happiness well beyond the finishing line of smoking with my father and my mother.

Irena Bauman

Smoke-filled rooms: photographs from the Bauman home

Karl Dudman

Outside the house my grandparents lived in stands a giant beech tree. Come the autumn months, like every beech in Leeds, it lets its leaves fall; the leaves don't jump and the tree doesn't push them, it simply stops holding on. A gust of wind or the beating of wings will pillage and scatter its brittle gold coins until just a bare frame remains. So it was when my grandfather died, and the house that for decades of family history had watched beech leaves fall loosened its own grip. In the stillness of this home, life's treasured detritus had built up over decades. Now, a slow current of family and friends through its dark rooms saw bits and pieces of the house dislodged and dispersed; carried in solemn hands to far corners. In the final waiting days of my grandfather's life, I watched as glasses started getting cleaned and surfaces dusted, and I realised with alarm that this process would begin more or less straight away. The stillness would soon be gone for ever. I felt a great urgency to return to Lawnswood Gardens with my camera, and carefully archive what I could of my grandparents' home before it was metabolised by the wider family and whitewashed for new residents. And this I did in the liminal weeks between death and its rituals, to perform my own act of remembrance; an album portrait of the house itself.

This was not merely a functional exercise in documenting space; training a wide-angle lens at the corner of each room like an estate agent preparing for sale. It was personal. As the youngest of the grandchildren, and the only British one never to have lived in Leeds, I felt that a relative poverty of shared time with my grandparents would leave me little of personal connection to carry them by. 'In this life of mine', writes my grandfather in his memoirs (soon to be published by Polity Press), 'I am the only resident. Only I can give an insider report. My memory of my life has no holes. If there were any, they would not belong to my life anyway.' In this sense, I felt the life that I call my own simply had less of him in it. And while years had bestowed on others beloved items, photos taken,

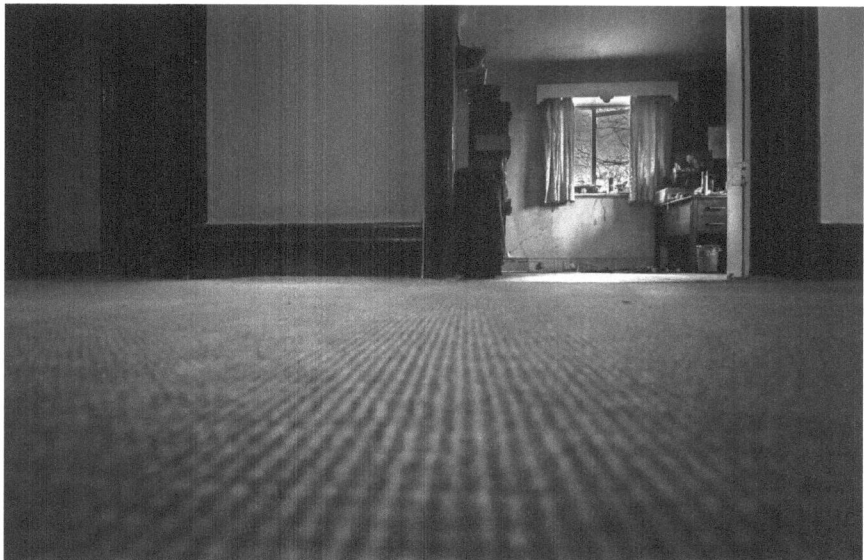

books dedicated, powerful words exchanged and deep memories, I could not borrow from others' biographies to write my own.

I knew then that this house held major significance for my relationship with my grandparents. For one thing, the holeless narrative my memory tells of them is one of complete domesticity. Both my grandparents had names, canons and physical bodies that traversed global distances, but it was never in far-flung lecture halls that I experienced them. I knew of their constant migrations, but it was always, inevitably, in the still and sedentary moments between that I saw them.

A dimly lit detached house in suburban Leeds, wrapped in a protective shroud of ivy; the heavy silence that filled the rooms during the hours of siesta; the feeling of a finger tracing an armchair's embossed paisleys while awaiting some plate loaded with salmon; the hurried bartering of food between my sister and me when his back was briefly turned ... these moments were my relationship with my grandparents made physical in the house. But when what is 'mine' is not a feeling, a remembered conversation, or something meaningful that can live on a shelf, but a house, an environment, something material, how does that vessel *stay* mine? How do I keep hold of it when it's gone? This was the hope behind the album; to return alone, and by the fading afterglow of my grandfather's presence, somehow commit this house's material life to photographic memory.

The perspective of the photos may be a visualisation of my own recollections, but the house itself was deeply memorious. The family moved to Leeds

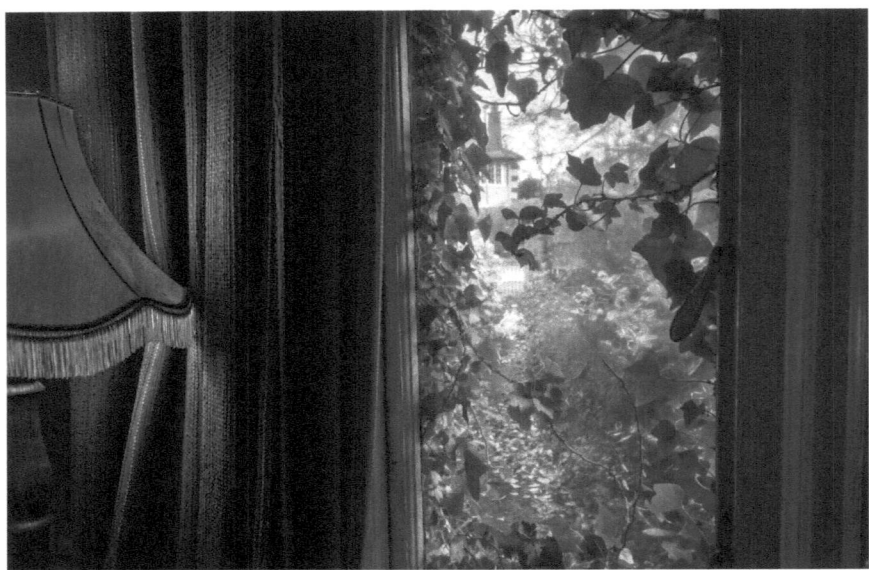

in 1971, and one felt that little had changed since those first days, beyond the natural forces of accumulation and decay. Indeed as I paced the house alone that January afternoon, forty-five years of family history presented themselves as a single frozen moment.

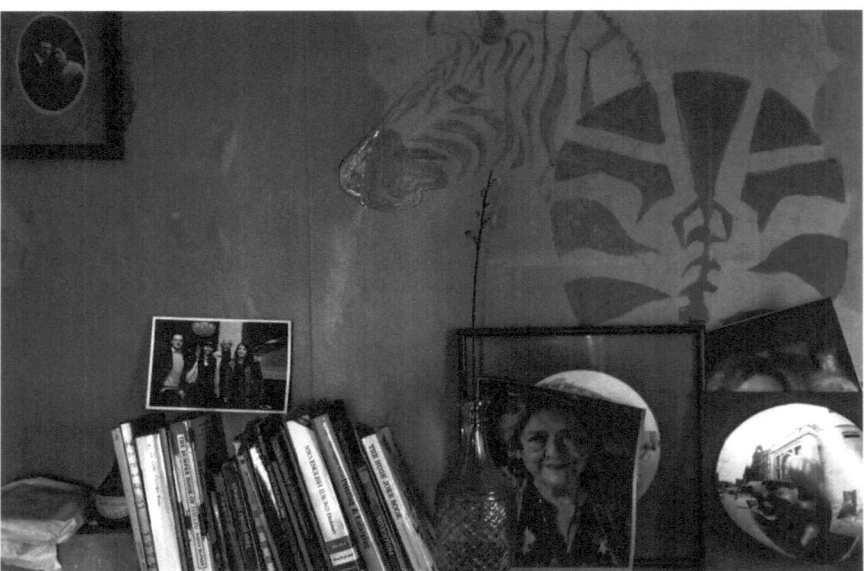

A painted zebra still adorned an upstairs wall, the nascent sign of my then teenage mother's artistic future. Elsewhere, decorations whose true colours I could only guess at, having been slowly repainted by decades of tobacco smoke.

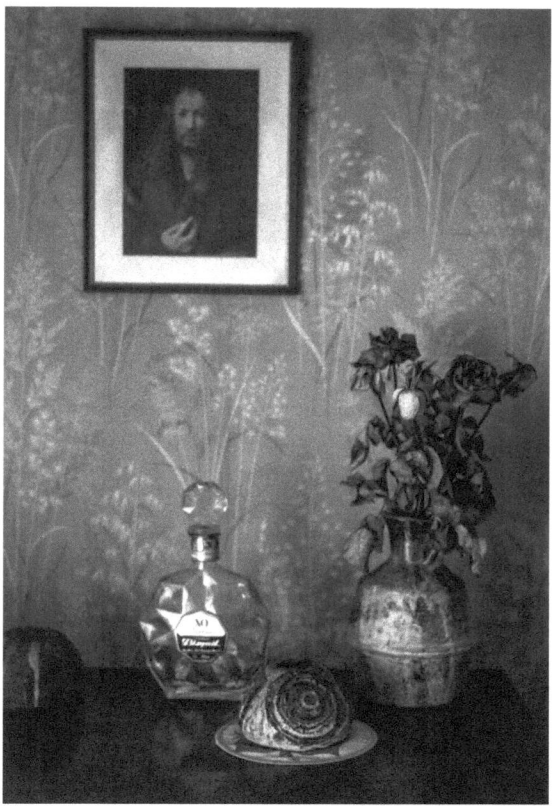

Dried flowers perched atop a chest of drawers. Who could say what year they had first pushed through the soil? To see these things was to dispel the abstraction of the past, to feel part of the mythology of the family.

It was not just what was visibly *present* in the house that was important. Like the photographic concept of negative space, the *un*seen and *un*spoken can hold their own prominence in one's mind and memory, and in Lawnswood Gardens everything was semi-buried, seen only in the half-light. The past was no exception. The lives of both my grandparents trailed through some of the most iconic yet ineffable moments in modern history, and in the stagnant silence of this home, the weight of that history felt distant but never absent; like a shape in the corner of one's vision. My grandfather's personal course through the Holocaust, the storming of Berlin, the turbulent evolution of Polish Communism, the

antisemitic purges of 1968 and subsequent Jewish diaspora was one so scruti-
nised and visible, both historically and individually. Yet somehow it always felt
elusive, murky and incomplete.

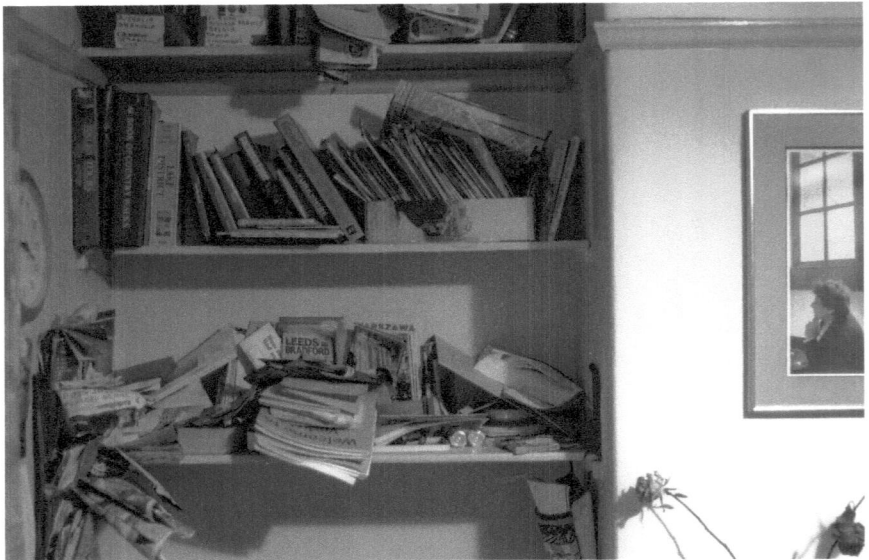

His mind, read by so many, buckled bookshelves the world over, and yet
held an inscrutability that often left even those closest to him guessing his true
thoughts. At times I even felt the air was charged with an unspoken politics.
Mysterious break-ins and targeted political confrontations periodically resurrected past violations of the family home in Poland. Fragments translated from
online fora with painful curiosity suggested he was still a useful bogeyman for
some on the Polish far-right. Despite its leafy anonymity, life at Lawnswood in
all these ways seemed to embody both the centre and the periphery, presence
and absence, noise and silence.

What became an interesting challenge for me in creating this album was
the fact that these contrasts had to come across not just in the atmosphere of
the house but in the way that space itself was conveyed. Just as my grandfather
straddled the boundary of the ultra-visible and the obscure, so too did this
boundary run visibly through the house. *Uwaga Pies*, read the sign above the
phone-booth-sized kitchen: 'beware the dog'.

Indeed, though communicated in rather less comical and explicit terms, the
house was tacitly divided into domains of varying degrees of access.

There were rooms I never once entered. Others held the proverbial 'hearth'
around which sociality gathered, but also doubled as a studio where the

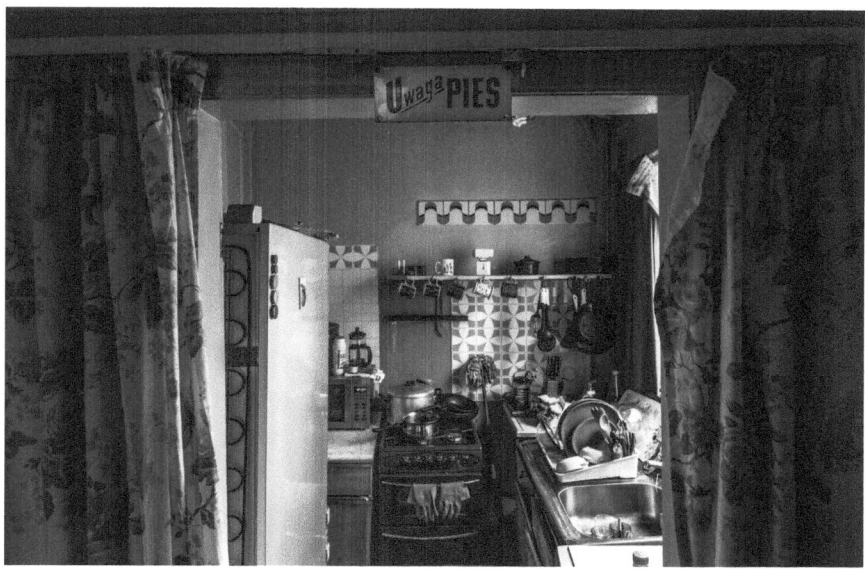

professor's persona would often be put on display for visiting discussants, journalists and photographers. Indeed, for a publication about Zygmunt Bauman's relationship with the photograph, there is no small discussion to be had about how he chose to feature in them. Smoke diffusing from a loaded pipe, the laurel wreath of bristling white hair, and an ever-shifting landscape of literature piled on haphazard surfaces and precarious DIY shelves; these were the signature props for a scholar fluent in the language of image. I grew up seeing that familiar book-strewn living room in national news outlets; it only more recently occurred to me how strange it was that I had never even seen the room where my grandfather slept. This was not just a man who cared about demarcating his public and private life, but one who skilfully cultivated and managed a play of hypervisibility and solitude as discrete as night and day. For me, the errant grandson let loose on the house in the master's absence, I have had to choose how much to affront that balance, first in taking the photographs and then in letting them be seen. Again, this album being more memorial than archive, it was a truer testament to let unknown rooms remain slivers of light through a cracked door.

Through this project and the thought I've given to it since, I have come to understand the house as a proxy for how he organised his own life and identity. Not only was it replete with material and sensory associations for me, it was a visible palimpsest of family history, and a stage on which my grandfather in particular could control what of himself he gave to the world, and what he kept for himself. Returning to these photographs after five years with a new

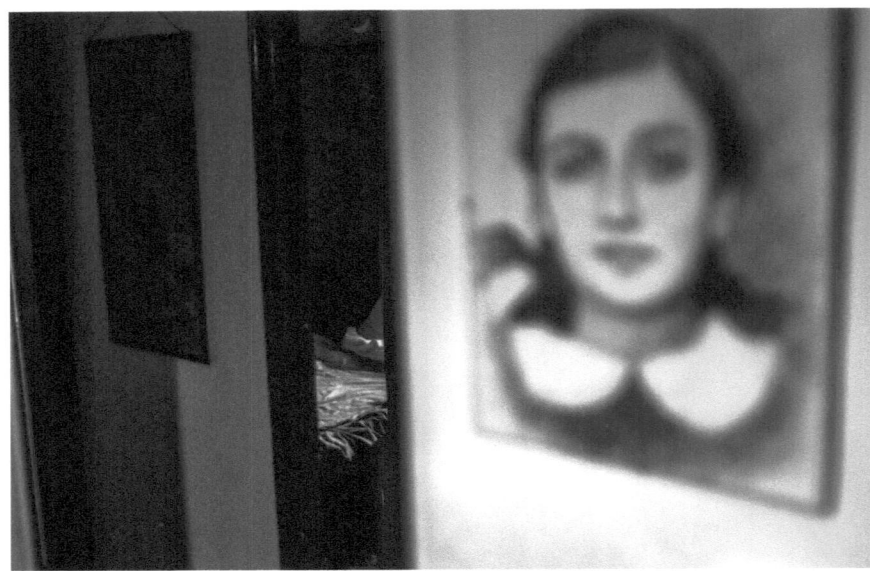

focus – i.e. his own photography – a new collection of objects call out for attention, previously buried in anonymity. The house was in fact everywhere adorned with photographs. Yet, depicting strange places and unmet faces, they had long ago joined the general background noise of the setting, alongside unknown authors and trinkets without biography.

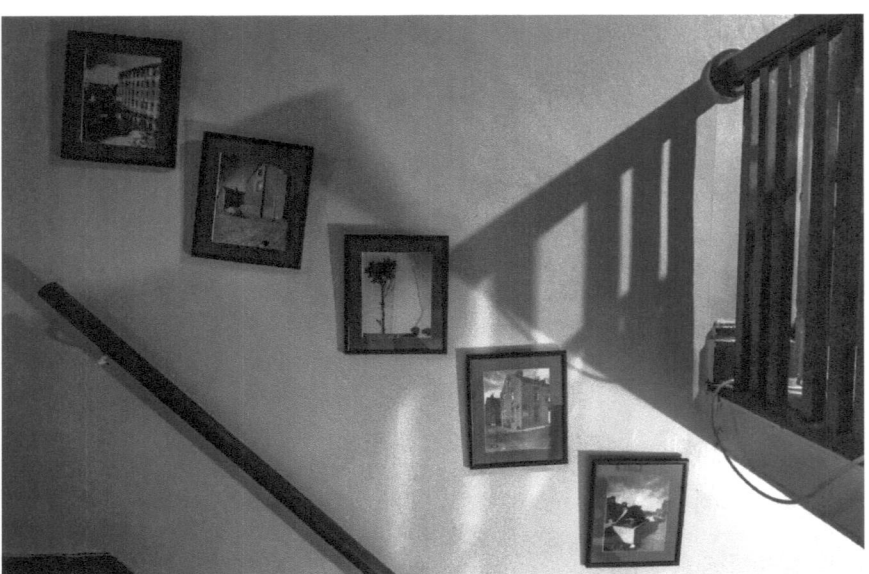

These images were buried to me, not just under years of dust and smoke, but also to my comprehension. My grandfather's homemade darkroom – still fitted with its last red bulb – had long disappeared under a disguise of cans, jams and biscuit tins.

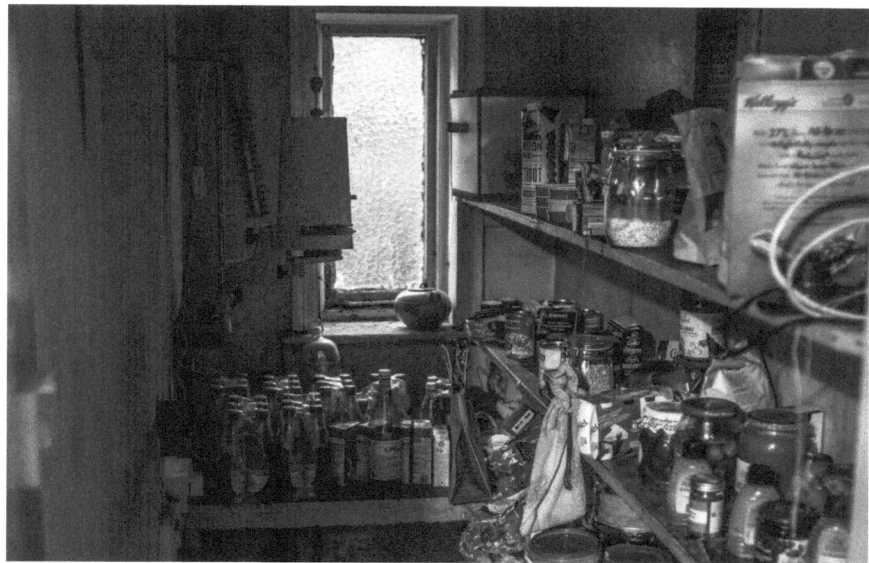

As another room I tacitly knew not to enter, it passed as a pantry for many years. Even the very fact of his one-time relationship with photography remained entirely unspoken. In 2010 I was asked to prepare a slideshow of his photographs that was to run on loop at the opening of the Bauman Institute at the University of Leeds. Being handed the selection of monochrome works was my first conscious encounter with Bauman the Photographer. But even from that point, and with the development of my own love of photography, it was a subject that did not arise in conversation.

In all senses then, getting to know his photography has been a kind of excavation. Much like the process of filling in the gaps of my grandmother's life upon reading her autobiographies, calibrating this catalogue of past work to the old man I knew as a grandfather entailed no small amount of guessing and reconciliation. Who, what and where were these unfamiliar subjects? Did he see photography as sociology made visible, or was it an unthinking exercise of aesthetic impulses? A rare clue came in the form of a brief foreword introducing his 1984 exhibition entitled 'Moods and Shapes'. In it, he suggests that photography inhabits 'the world ... of *familiar* thoughts and *familiar* feelings' and that its meanings are derived more from what the viewer recognises than what the photographer intends. It was in reading this that I felt a convergence between my thoughts in capturing the world within walls of the house, and his the society beyond. It was precisely Lawnswood's 'known shapes' and 'lived-through moods' that I hoped – through photography – to keep for myself long after layers of magnolia paint have purged the walls of their memory and made the place placeless. And because those shapes and moods are not contained within the image but activated 'in dialogue with the viewer', this album is in effect something my grandparents and I made together.

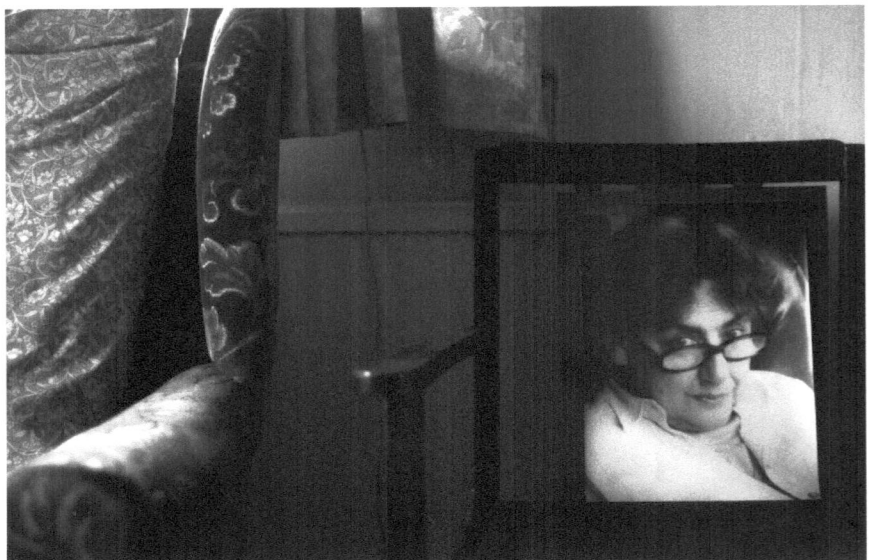

Fittingly then, it has been in the language my grandfather and I shared – that of photography – that this work of remembrance gets his tenuous blessing to fulfil its purpose.

The album has become, for me, an intimate and inalienable act of collaborative storytelling and a place where my memories of my grandparents can live. The beauty of Bauman the Photographer's message, however, is that this is not lost through being shared. Like a mirror that presents a tailored image to every viewer, these photographs carry different meaning and association for all who look at them. Family, friend, acquaintance, visitor, stranger. All can find their own moods and shapes in the half-light; my grandparents fading into the gloom with each concentric layer of intimacy, until a chair is just a chair, a house a house, a beech tree a beech tree …

Acknowledgements

Our first and most heartfelt thanks go to members of the Bauman family, and in particular Zygmunt and Janina's daughters, Anna Sfard, Irena Bauman and Lydia Bauman. They supported this project from the beginning, and have been enthusiastic and encouraging all along. We thank Irena especially for providing many of the photographs in this book by taking the time to go through the private family archive, and then arranging to have good copies made. Thanks to Lydia for allowing us to reprint her 2010 catalogue essay in this volume. It's also a real delight for us, as editors, to have seven members of the next generation of Baumans included in the book – six grandchildren and one grandson-in-law. We have very much enjoyed working with them over the past eighteen months. We also very much appreciate the support and encouragement of Aleksandra Kania, Zygmunt's late-life companion and second wife.

We are indebted to the Bauman Institute and the University of Leeds for a number of things. Director Adrian Favell encouraged his colleagues to collaborate with us; Mark Davis (founding director of the Institute) was instrumental in acquiring university funds to facilitate open-access publication; and Jack Palmer has been enormously helpful throughout, starting with going to the trouble of taking snapshots of Bauman's photos in the Institute archive so we had something to work with. Tim Procter and the staff in Special Collections at the university helped us arrange to get the copies we needed of many of the photos included here.

We were keen to include Keith Tester's essay on Bauman and film, and are very grateful to his widow Linda and daughter Maddy in agreeing to this and in sending material from Keith's files.

Thank you to Monika Krajewska for permission to reproduce her photographs in the reprinted 1989 essay by Zygmunt Bauman, and for sending us images for our use. That essay was originally published in the *Jewish Quarterly*, and we thank the journal for permission to reprint. Thanks also to the *Polish Sociological Review* for permission to reproduce Keith Tester's 2014 essay.

Both the editors have published with Manchester University Press before, and here join together in thanking our editor Matthew Frost and all the team at the Press for their work on the book, especially Alun Richards, David Appleyard and copy-editor John Banks.

Many of the photographs in this book are reproduced with the permission of Special Collections, Leeds University Library (shelf marks MS 2067/B/10 and MS 2067/B/2/4).

Thank you to John Schwarzmantel for allowing us to include the portrait of his parents.

Photos in Karl Dudman's essay are © Karl Dudman, and are published with his permission.

The first photo in the long essay by Antony Bryant and Griselda Pollock is their own.

All other photos in the book are © Zygmunt Bauman, and are published with the permission of the Bauman family. All the photos are undated and untitled, apart from the cover image.

We are very grateful to the editors of *Thesis Eleven* for financial support in relation to costs of image reproduction in this book and to the Bauman Institute and the University of Leeds for financial support towards the cost of publication.

Contributors

Irena Bauman is an architect and an urban designer practising from Leeds. Her practice and research are concerned with how architecture and architectural thinking can facilitate local communities to mitigate, adapt and become more resilient to the uncertainties that lie ahead. She co-designs with communities and a wide range of stakeholders and often collaborates with artists in tackling complex issues of ownership, consensus and justice.

Lydia Bauman is an artist and art historian, graduate of the Courtauld Institute of Art in London. She divides her time between painting in her London studio, exhibiting widely and lecturing, including at the National Gallery in London, Tate and National Portrait Gallery and for culture tour companies such as Martin Randall Travel. Lydia is one of three daughters of Janina and Zygmunt Bauman.

Alex Bauman-Lyons is an architect and design director. After graduating from Newcastle and Westminster Universities he has lived and worked internationally in London, New York and Buenos Aires. He currently works for a pan-European property developer specialising in the hospitality sector. He lives in Hackney, London, with his partner and two children. Alex is the grandchild of Janina and Zygmunt Bauman.

Hana Bauman-Lyons was born in Leeds and graduated from the University of the West of England in Bristol. She worked for ten years in London's creative industries before relocating to Leeds. She now runs her own company selling vintage homeware and design pieces sourced from across Europe with a strong focus on and interest in ceramics. She is the granddaughter of Zygmunt and Janina Bauman.

Peter Beilharz is Professor of Critical Theory at Sichuan University in China. He is also Emeritus Professor of Sociology at La Trobe University, Melbourne. He is founding editor of *Thesis Eleven*, and has published thirty books, most recently *Intimacy in Postmodern Times – A Friendship with Zygmunt Bauman* (2020), *Circling Marx* (2020) and *The Work of History*, edited with Sian Supski (2022).

Antony Bryant is Professor of Informatics at Leeds Beckett University, and Chief Researcher, Institute of Education Research, Vytautas Magnus University, Lithuania. Publications include *Grounded Theory and Grounded Theorizing: Pragmatism in Research Practice* (2017) and, edited with Kathy Charmaz, *The SAGE Handbook of Grounded Theory* (2007) and *The Sage Handbook of Current Developments in Grounded Theory* (2019).

Karl Dudman is a writer, photographer and the youngest grandchild of Zygmunt and Janina Bauman. His past work, exhibited at London's Mall Galleries and published in print and online, has focused on the relationships between people and their natural environments. Karl is currently undertaking his PhD in anthropology at the University of Oxford, where he researches alternative understandings of climate change denial in rural North Carolina.

Ben Hepworth is Janina and Zygmunt's grandson-in-law. He is married to Sofia and they live in Leeds with their daughter Alicia. He enjoyed regular visits to Lawnswood Gardens, to sample Zygmunt's home cooking alongside conversation and televised sport. Ben is a mathematician: he completed his PhD at the University of Leeds before joining the Government Operational Research Service.

Sofia Hepworth is Janina and Zygmunt's granddaughter. She moved to Leeds having grown to love the city from frequent visits to her grandparents. She studied for a BA in French and Management – including a year in Paris – at the University of Leeds, followed by an MA in Global Development. Sofia continues to live in Leeds with her husband Ben and their daughter Alicia, and now works at the University.

Jack Palmer is a Senior Lecturer in Sociology at Leeds Trinity University and is deputy director of the Bauman Institute. His most recent publications include *Zygmunt Bauman and the West: A Sociology of Intellectual Exile* (2023) and, co-edited with Dariusz Brzeziński, *Revisiting Modernity and the Holocaust: Heritage, Dilemmas, Extensions* (2022).

Griselda Pollock is Professor Emerita of Social and Critical Histories of Art at the University of Leeds, where she taught postcolonial, feminist, queer and social histories of art and cultural studies She is the 2020 Laureate of the Holberg Prize. Recent publications include *Charlotte Salomon in the Theatre of Memory* (2018) and *Killing Men & Dying Women: Imagining Difference in 1950s New York Painting* (2022).

Anna Sfard is a Professor Emerita at the University of Haifa, Israel. She conducts research and teaches in the domain of learning sciences. As reflected in the title of one of her books, *Thinking as Communicating: Human Development, the Growth of Discourses, and Mathematizing*, the main theme of her scholarship is the relation between cognition and communication. Anna is one of Zygmunt and Janina Bauman's three daughters.

Emi Sfard is an Israeli painter, illustrator and new-media artist. Her art addresses political and social issues and is presented in galleries and museums around Israel. With degrees in industrial design and creative art, she also works as an instructor for mentally struggling artists and has designed diverse products for kids and illustrated several children's books. She is the granddaughter of Zygmunt and Janina Bauman.

Michael Sfard is an Israeli human rights lawyer specialising in international human rights law and the laws of war. He serves as the legal adviser to several Israeli human rights and humanitarian organizations as well as Palestinian communities and activists. He frequently publishes opinion pieces in the Israeli and international press and is the author of several books including *The Wall and The Gate: Israel, Palestine and the Legal Battle for Human Rights* (2018). He is the Baumans' grandson.

Sian Supski is a cultural sociologist who works as a journeywoman researcher. She has written two books, *A Proper Foundation: A History of the Lotteries Commission of Western Australia* and *It was Another Skin: The Kitchen in 1950s Western Australia*. She is an editor of *Thesis Eleven*. Sian was a visiting scholar at the Stellenbosch Institute for Advanced Study in 2015 and is affiliated with Sichuan University. She is Adjunct Research Fellow, La Trobe University.

Keith Tester (1960–2019) was Professor of Cultural Sociology at the University of Portsmouth and Professor of Sociology at the University of Hull. His many books include *Animals and Society* (1991), *Civil Society* (1992), *Moral Culture* (1997) and *Eric Rohmer: Film as Theology* (2008). A close friend of the Baumans, he published a number of books on Zygmunt, including *Conversations with Zygmunt Bauman* (2001) and *The Social Thought of Zygmunt Bauman* (2004).

Izabela Wagner is a sociologist (PhD from EHESS – School for Advanced Studies in Social Sciences in Paris), Professor of Sociology at Collegium Civitas University in Warsaw, a fellow at the French Collaborative Institute on Migrations in Paris, and Associate Researcher at Sophiapol (Paris X University) in France. She is the author of *Producing Excellence: The Making of Virtuosos* (2015) and *Bauman: A Biography* (2020).

Janet Wolff is Professor Emerita in the School of Arts, Languages and Cultures at the University of Manchester. She has also taught at the University of Leeds, the University of Rochester (USA) and Columbia University. She is the author of a number of books on aesthetics and the sociology of art. Her most recent book is a memoir/social history, *Austerity Baby*, published by Manchester University Press in 2017.

Notes on photographs

All photographs © Zygmunt Bauman unless otherwise noted.

All photographs untitled unless otherwise noted.

There is no systematic archive of Bauman's photos, and no detailed record of his exhibitions, or of which pictures he exhibited in different shows. We have gathered photographs from the Bauman Institute's collection, from family members and from other private owners of portraits and other photos.

EU authorised representative for GPSR:
Easy Access System Europe, Mustamäe tee 50,
10621 Tallinn, Estonia
gpsr.requests@easproject.com